Dyslexia: Prove teachers and experts WRONG!

by

Joseph Kennedy

Free your child's spirit and Intellect.
Dramatically improve reading and spelling through systematic imprinting and automatic letter selection.

Over 50 years of successful Implementation.

Contents:

Part	Heading	Page
-	Foreword	3
1	Why school and therapies cannot really help children	5
2	A single brain region and a pile of letters. The true cause of dyslexia – and the only effective solution	20
3	"Is my child really dyslexic?" How to identify dyslexia reliably	40
4	Type your way to success! How your child can improve by up to three grades in dictation and essays, homework and foreign languages	60
5	Alphabet soup Games for better marks	82
6	"Okay! Mother, I can do it!" How to motivate your child	98
7	Partners or adversaries? How to get teachers on board – without capsizing	131
8	Five and six ... are nine? Dyslexia and dyscalculia	155
9	"Why is my child so inattentive?" Dyslexia and attention deficit	177
	Postscript That's enough for now. Time to play......	206
	Dedication and thanks	207
	About the author	208

Foreword

Dear Reader,

The book you are holding in your hands describes a proven method for overcoming reading and spelling difficulties, a condition known as *dyslexia*. I have been applying this method for 30 years now in the *Kennedy Tutorial School*, and the results speak for themselves. Children can improve their reading and writing skills considerably and, in general, overcome their dyslexia completely within a year with only 20 minutes of practise a day. As a consequence, they no longer experience the same degree of pressure in school, rediscover the pleasure of reading and have more leisure time to enjoy.

At the *Kennedy Tutorial School* in Tuttlingen, where children suffering from dyslexia, dyscalculia (and often adhd) receive targeted encouragement and support, we offer parents a firm guarantee: their money back plus €100 if our method fails to achieve success. This offer has only been taken up on three occasions since the school was established.

Neuropsychologist and child psychiatrist Fritz Held, who was involved in developing the essential features of this method, had applied it with success for over 35 years in his practice. Developing his method further, I supplemented it with a variety of playful exercises which children enjoy and are even more effective in achieving the desired results. This book therefore represents a total of 65 years and more of *practical experience*, experience from which you can benefit. Take advantage of it!

The method described here is not scientifically proven, probably because it is so simple and not consistent with conventional educational research and efforts to address the problem of dyslexia.

Nevertheless, it is extremely effective. It is up to you to apply it in an unbiased and resolute manner, putting it into practise in everyday life. Don't let the routine of daily school life dissuade you from sticking to this method on a day-to-day level. Your child will thank you for it.

I hope you enjoy this playful approach to effectively and measurably overcoming the problem of dyslexia, and I wish you every success in your efforts!

Please note that this book is written in Oxford English. Also, I refer throughout to the decimal marking system that is used in Germany and is graded from 1.0 to 6.0, as follows:

1.0 Excellent	2.0 Good	3.0 Satisfactory
4.0 Sufficient; a Pass	5.0 Insufficient	6.0 Very poor

Enjoy the reading!

Joseph Kennedy

1.   Why school and therapies cannot really help children

"Is this dyslexia, or within the norm?" Frau Novak and Herr Weiss are sitting in the staff room of *Maria Theresia* primary school. Decisions were being made on which pupils to allow to participate in the dyslexia remedial course. The problem was where exactly to draw the line for each child.

"Hmm, it's hard to say. Let's take a look at the obvious cases first." Herr Weiss places an exercise book on the desk and opened it. "Just look at Arthur's last dictation. 100 words and 30 errors! His previous dictations weren't any better, and you'd think he was still in the 2nd class if you heard the mistakes he makes when reading. But he's in the 4th class! He manages only a 5 in German."

"Yes, well, that's a clear case", agreed Frau Novak. "But the course would be full then. What's going on with Kirstin?"

Kirstin was the problem child in Frau Novak's class. Although she only made half as many mistakes in dictation as Arthur, the number was really too high. When Frau Novak asked her if she read at home, she simply shook her head in silence.

"I think she's just lazy", remarked Herr Weiss. "I've got her in English, but she hardly ever does her homework and in class she just sits there showing absolutely no sign of interest."

"That could be because she's having difficulties with reading. Couldn't that be the problem?", countered Frau Novak. "Could we make an exception and increase the course to eight participants?"

Herr Weiss played with his pen, then placed it down with a loud clack on the desk. "The parents of the other children who have similar difficulties won't like that. She'll just have to practise more at home, there's no other way around it."

Helpless helper

The situation facing children with dyslexia in Germany has improved considerably in recent decades – or at least superficially. Most, though not all teachers, are at least familiar with the problem and no longer brand pupils who make a lot of spelling mistakes and are poor readers as merely stupid or lazy. Children with dyslexia can obtain support outside normal tuition hours.

However, the chances of obtaining help are not good for pupils whose problems in reading and writing are less obvious. Placements in support courses are simply allocated starting with the poorest performing pupils in a class and moving upwards. Rather than deciding whether dyslexia exists on the basis of objective criteria and if the support provided is expedient, pupils are simply compared with each other.

I regard this as unprofessional, but it is hardly surprising, given that not every teacher is trained to identify dyslexia! The issue is far too complex to be introduced to candidates in the teaching profession over a weekend seminar. Literature addressing dyslexia is so complicated that even committed teachers despair when it comes to the question of how best to proceed. Experts differ greatly when it comes to defining dyslexia, and an extremely broad variety of theories exists regarding its causes and potential remedies.

There is even enormous uncertainty over the number of children affected. Estimates range from four to 20 per cent of all schoolchildren, according to the German association for dyslexia and dyscalculia (*Bundesverband Legasthenie und Dyskalkulie*). Consequently, teachers who wish to provide the best possible help for their pupils are themselves often helpless and perplexed. They are forced to make decisions without the requisite basic information.

In practise, it seems that each school can decide for itself today whether a child is dyslexic or not. The term "dyslexic" is only used with reservation in this book. Fundamentally speaking, a lot of restraint should be exercised when applying such labels, because these can all too easily follow those affected for their entire lives and lead to their marginalisation.

However, schools are not completely on their own in this respect, as they can call on the assistance of specialists (referred to as dyslexia experts in Baden-Württemberg, Germany the state in which I live).

So, is it all very professionally organised after all? Not quite, because many schools do not have dyslexia experts due to a shortage of such personnel. Schools are authorised to employ a very simple criterion when it comes to reaching decisions. As of late, all children in Baden-Württemberg who obtain a mark worse than 4 in German are considered "dyslexic" according to state law. The school then decides whether individual pupils should be given additional support in German. This depends on the degree to which dyslexia is evident. The yardstick is generally set high with, for example, the child needing to suffer from both reading and spelling difficulties. They are also compared to other pupils. In other words, the child needs to be considerably worse at reading and writing than other pupils to be evaluated and recognised as dyslexic.

This procedure frequently means that a child who reads poorly and/or regularly makes numerous spelling mistakes does not receive any particular support from the school. This questionable selection procedure for the "chosen few" to receive help continues to an even greater degree in the secondary stage. It is well known that in lower secondary schools (Hauptschulen), the vast majority of children make numerous spelling mistakes and rarely pick up a book because their dyslexia robs them of any pleasure in this respect. This really comes as no surprise, as very many children attend a school of this kind due to their poor performance in German (and mathematics). However, poor marks in these subjects frequently have little to do with the child's intelligence, being rather the result of dyslexia or dyscalculia or both.

Put bluntly, one could say that lower secondary schools are merely collecting points for dyslexics! This leads to a bizarre situation if a decision needs to be made at a lower secondary school (whose pupils are almost all suffering from dyslexia or dyscalculia) about which children should attend a remedial course.

The situation is particularly extreme at special needs schools for children with learning difficulties (also referred to simply as special schools), with classes consisting exclusively of children suffering from dyslexia and dyscalculia. But dyslexia is not enough to be "accepted" at a special needs school. In addition to dyslexia and dyscalculia, very many pupils at these schools suffer from considerable concentration disorders and suspected attention-deficit hyperactivity disorder (ADHD).

The special school aims to help children with learning disabilities to a degree that could allow them to move up again into a regular school. Unfortunately, however, this outcome is achieved far too rarely. Instead of continuing to work on the causes and alleviation of dyslexia, the focus today is more on integrative and inclusive education systems. An integrative school system allows children with a variety of different requirements to learn together, meaning in this context, that special needs pupils can be placed in the same classroom with other primary and lower secondary school pupils.

To ensure that inclusion functions, the individual pupil with special needs requires assistance with, for example, reading and lettering to help him or her keep up with the rest of the class. The advantages of this approach are obvious. The self-esteem of pupils who previously felt excluded improves ("I belong here too!"). However, the demands made on the teacher increase considerably. They need to plan and organise tuition that takes the learning requirements of *all* pupils into consideration. They also need to coordinate with the special needs teacher providing remedial tuition for pupils requiring support (an allocation of 2.5 hours a week in Baden-Württemberg).

The class teacher needs to take increasing care of a class where differences of this nature are not always resolved peacefully. Pupils who perform better are at a disadvantage, as the teacher has less time for them, and it is to be feared that the general level of performance of the class will fall. It is also doubtful whether this special needs model provides pupils with adequate support, as the specialised teacher only sees them for two and a half hours a week and the class teacher is not trained to address their special needs.

This problem is also encountered in remedial courses for dyslexia offered at schools generally.

Learning and cramming ... – and still only a 6!

Michael looked at his dictation and groaned. 22 mistakes, and a 6 for his trouble! That meant five more mistakes than his last unpractised dictation! He stood up and went over to the teacher.

"Herr Schmider, I've been on this course for months! Now I've got five more mistakes that in my last dictation. What's going on here?", he complained.

Herr Schmider looked kindly at him. "We've got to stick at it. If you continue to practise according to the plan, we made together for you, things will work out one day", he assured him in an attempt at encouragement.

"Yeah, sure", said Michael, lowering his head and returning reluctantly to his seat. He rested his head in both hands and stared straight ahead. Herr Schmider noticed how Michael's tears fell onto the desk. He shook his head helplessly.

Why, despite remedial tuition, do pupils fail to improve? The explanation possibly lies in the fact that the remedial tuition received is inadequate. Can *one* hour a week really achieve anything? This single hour only offers enough time to repeat the subject matter with which children are actually already familiar but have failed to master. This is frustrating for all participants.

I also suspect that the problem is not only the amount of remedial tuition, but the *nature* of it.

Teachers often employ an educational concept which, in itself, is sound. Together with each pupil, they analyse the individual weaknesses and address typical faults. If, for example, a child demonstrates a weakness when it comes to upper- and lower-case letters, the parts of speech are discussed and upper- and lower-case letters practised. If the weakness relates to correct sequencing of the various letters, the teacher then explains the appropriate rules and lets the pupil practise these repeatedly.

This approach is, in principle, practical if a child has knowledge gaps in the subject matter, such as spelling mistakes made because the child does not understanding certain rules of grammar. However, dyslexia has absolutely nothing to do with *understanding*. Dyslexia sufferers are just as intelligent as other people and usually have no difficulty in understanding the theory behind rules. They are just unable to apply them. Targeted training to tackle "weak points" can even be counterproductive, because the child may improve somewhat in areas covered, but then make additional mistakes elsewhere.

Countless reading exercises will not whet the appetite of children for voluntary reading; the ratio of effort to reading pleasure is just too meagre in the case of these children.

To sum up, it could be said that conventional remedial courses just do not work for dyslexia. Therefore, would it help at all if teachers of remedial courses received training in highly specific methods to alleviate dyslexia sufferers of their pain?

No time for dyslexia

There was a definite shortage of space in my office. Not really surprising, as Frau Winkler, the principal of a lower secondary school (*Hauptschule*), her vice-principal, a few teachers, parents, the chairwoman of the parents' council, Frau März, and two trainee teachers had been invited to the meeting. Karin Mink, educational director at the *Kennedy Tutorial School*, sat beside me, and Elke Margreiter, our PR lady, was also in attendance. Eleven people in *a single* room. And we all agreed that the idea was worth giving a shot.

The delegation from the lower secondary school had been with us for an entire afternoon, beginning with tuition for dyslexia training and then attending a class for children suffering from dyscalculia. Frau Winkler now wanted to introduce our methods in her school. Her two trainee teachers would take charge of the remedial courses.

"It sounds interesting", said one of them, her eyes lighting up. "I'm looking forward to seeing if we can accomplish the same results as you."

"So are we", said Frau Margreiter. "Please be so kind as to record any improvements achieved, and collect feedback from the parents. Ask their permission to publish any endorsements they may make and forward them to us. We can then post them on our website."

"We'll provide you with the tuition material you need, and we'll be more than happy to help you further. If you have any questions, don't hesitate to call me", said Frau Mink.

An exchange of know-how and tuition material for details of marks achieved and parental recommendations as feedback is a win-win situation for both parties.

"And if you're successful, please recommend us to other schools and professional circles", I added.

"You can count on it", one father promised. "We've been cramming for sometimes hours every day with our Tobias for over a year, but without any success. His spelling is poor and he still doesn't pick up a book of his own accord. We're pretty desperate now. If your method helps us further, we promise to spread the news!"

We had rarely experienced the level of enthusiasm expressed by these professionals and parents. A staff member from the research department of a university who wanted to conduct a scientific study of this trial in a pilot project, was also present! Having agreed on further preparations for the coming weeks, we were now ready to get started.

Funny enough, things then went very quiet for a long period.

One day, I received an email from Frau Winkler that simply stated: "I'm sorry to inform you that the planned courses for dyslexia and dyscalculia cannot be held. They just can't be fitted into the timetable. Our trainee teachers have their hands full with normal tuition. I'm very sorry to have to tell you this."

Committed school principals and teachers who wish to help children with learning difficulties frequently fail due to system-related factors. The problem is commonly that the allocation of material and the timetable are already overstressed and there is simply a shortage of personnel.

I have often seen the introduction of remedial tuition for children with dyslexia and dyscalculia come to nothing for these reasons – despite the enormous interest expressed by teachers and parents.

In only two cases did a teacher succeed in actually introducing these kinds of courses in cooperation with us, but in both they were restricted to a period of three months. Interestingly enough, they involved schools for children with learning disabilities, one of which was a vocational school. The startling improvements achieved were clearly measurable, but further cooperation failed because additional demands of this nature were not foreseen in the timetable. It proved possible to set up the courses at short notice as a project, but not as a long-term endeavour.

Only a mere fraction of children suffering from dyslexia can be provided with help under practical conditions because, quite simply, staff levels are inadequate. The principal is forced to organise remedial tuition lessons as best as possible, even though the hours required for these are just not available in most cases. This is due to inadequate funding of supplementary activities.

In addition to remedial courses for pupils with dyslexia and dyscalculia, these supplementary activities also include lessons dedicated to pupils who exhibit behavioural problems. Incidentally, behavioural disorders are frequently a consequence of learning difficulties, as those children affected are unable to keep up in lessons, become bored or irritated and demonstrate this through defiance, aggression and/or resignation. Moreover, a variety of activities involving group work (such as the school orchestra) need to be financed from the same budget, and these compete directly with remedial courses. A tough struggle ensues for the allocation of limited funds, which is why a considerable number of principals give preference to other activities before considering remedial courses for learning difficulties. The result is a near absence of remedial courses for dyslexia in all schools.

However, a shortage of funds is not the only reason for lack of action.

"My child isn't stupid!"

At the suggestion of parents who knew our work, I was once invited to speak on the subject of dyslexia and dyscalculia at an elite private school. The teachers were extremely enthusiastic but, despite this, the dyslexia courses never took place. The father who had initiated this contact wrote to tell me why:

"The school itself fears being seen as entertaining the 'unprofessional opinion' that the children affected are merely 'special-needs cases'. As it considers itself to be an elite school, dyslexia courses just don't fit the image. (...)

In addition, there are without a doubt many parents who, being unfamiliar with the causes of dyslexia, worry that they may have a stupid child - and that's something they don't want to parade before everybody. Many of them are business people who assume that their child will succeed them, and revealing that the child has difficulties would only tarnish the image of the business."

In other words: dyslexia courses are not held because parents are hesitant to admit that their child has dyslexia. And the school does not want to gain the reputation of being a refuge for problem cases. The preconception that dyslexia and dyscalculia have something to do with a lack of intelligence is apparently still widespread. Instead of coming to grips with the challenge, the problem is preferably swept under the carpet rather than suffering any potential loss of image. This attitude is exceedingly short-sighted, and unfortunately not restricted to uninformed parents and school managements. Even official directives issued by educational authorities would lead one to believe that the problem of dyslexia is being avoided.

The fact is that less dictation is demanded in primary schools is not new at all. According to a *Focus Schule Online* 10 January 2011, dictation is no longer permissible in the educational plan in Hamburg for assessing spelling ability. Martin Fix, language teacher and Rector of the Ludwigsburg University of Education, claims in the same report that dictation is not a suitable source of information on the spelling competence of a child.

This of course makes life very easy for pupils, parents and teachers. The average mark of a child improves without unpractised dictation, as it generally performs better doing essays and grammar than when having to spell less familiar texts correctly. In the case of essay-writing, the (rigorous) checking of spelling may vary depending on the school involved.

Quite a few primary schools (also outside of Hamburg) safeguard themselves even further by only allowing the writing of *practised* dictation. This is repeated and practised until almost every child can write it without any mistakes. This performance is a product of natural memory and has less to do with the child's spelling abilities per se. The average number of mistakes in *unpractised* dictation or self-composed texts is the *true* indicator of the level of spelling skills.

However, *practised* dictation ensures that considerably more pupils obtain a good mark – but not all! The reason this 'method' is ineffective for some is because in pronounced cases of dyslexia, even practised texts learnt completely by heart cannot always be recalled without errors.

This new approach was probably born of many bitter and unpleasant arguments between parents and teachers in the past. Where more *unpractised* dictation was written, the child regularly received poor marks. The level of performance was obvious – and along with this the improbability of the child moving up to a higher class, not to mention an intermediate (*Realschule*) or advanced (*Gymnasium*) secondary school. Every effort was, of course, made to avoid sending the child to a lower secondary school (*Hauptschule*), and a special needs school was unthinkable. Just to clarify any confusion:

Dictation is an instrument for evaluating the performance of a child when it comes to spelling, but no more than that. It is designed to indicate whether and where a learning deficit still exists, the aim being to enable the child to improve its spelling thus making as few mistakes as possible.

Dispensing with this control instrument is a sign of surrender, as it indicates that educational authorities, teachers and parents have grown to accept that our school system is incapable of teaching all children to spell correctly.

The next step was the introduction of a free choice of secondary schools for parents, up to and including grammar school. 11 of 16 German federal states had accomplished this by April 2013. So there has been a continuing reduction in the number of children attending lower secondary schools, and therefore more pupils than ever exhibiting dyslexia at intermediate and advanced secondary schools.

On the one hand, this is the consequence of a redistribution of pupils. However, it is also because the number of pupils affected by 'late-stage' dyslexia increases as a result. The introduction of the first or second foreign language can cause the reading and spelling function to collapse. Pupils whose ability to spell is somewhat weak, but adequate in their mother tongue, are often completely overtaxed on the introduction of a first or, certainly, a second foreign language. Typically, they make many mistakes in the reading and spelling of the foreign language, and this effect may even then begin to exhibit itself in their native script. Overburdened by dissimilar spelling rules in different languages, they suddenly begin to make mistakes in their mother language. As a consequence, a previously latent or marginal dyslexia often reveals itself following the move to an intermediate or advanced secondary school and the introduction of foreign languages.

So, the problem of dyslexia has suddenly had a massive impact on and in these secondary schools, and this development has also triggered various reactions – and none of them good. The motto is all too obvious – if you can't solve a problem, bypass it. Nowadays, dictation is rarely written in German and never in English. In the past, English dictation was regarded as a class test in its own right, being conducted and evaluated several times a year. Today, intermediate secondary schools in the Tuttlingen district usually make provisions for dictation in English as one of several parts of a single class test. Subsequently: spelling plays an increasingly subordinate role in foreign languages coupled with a higher evaluation of oral performance.

This cover-up goes even further, with up to 25 per cent of marking of the intermediate secondary examination (*Mittlere Reife*) consisting of the oral examination. Although it is assuredly desirable that pupils should not only read and write English well, but also speak it competently, sacrificing one goal for the benefit of the other is no solution, as many despairing employers can confirm.

Is there no way to protect children suffering from dyslexia without demanding too little of other pupils? Perhaps.

The "equilibrium of advantages" Or: the same opportunity for everyone.

Hans' excited voice was clearly audible from the hallway. "Mama, I've got my *Abitur*! "The young man ran into the kitchen, hugged his mother tightly and said: "Thanks, Mama, thanks for everything!"

And she had indeed done a lot to make this dream come true. The *Abitur* is the higher education entrance certificate in Germany, comparable to the International Baccalaureate. While Hans was at primary school, an open-minded teacher informed his mother that he probably suffered from dyslexia – just like his two older brothers. The diagnosis was confirmed by a specialised psychologist.

Following this, Hans' mother put herself forward for the parents' council at her children's school and remained in this office at the primary and advanced secondary school until Hans had reached the final (12th) class. In addition to her enormous commitment, she also became known for being well-informed when it came to educational rules and regulations. Armed with the psychologist's appraisal, she managed to ensure that the rule regarding "equilibrium of advantage" was applied to her three sons. Their performances with regard to spelling were generously evaluated, including also foreign languages. Hans' brothers had already passed the *Abitur* in this manner, and now, filled with pride, it was Hans' turn to show his mother his certificate.

"Look, Mama, I got 11 points in the oral test in German and, overall, an average of eight, and I even got nine points in English."

Just like his brothers, Hans would now have the chance to study. His future was secured.

Where a pronounced case of dyslexia cannot be bypassed through a broad-scale abandonment of dictation, a further option exists for parents in Germany: the 'equilibrium of advantage' (der Nachteilsausgleich). The rules regarding this differ from state to state within Germany. In Baden-Württemberg, for example, if children are proven to suffer from dyslexia, performances in reading and spelling in German and foreign languages must be generously evaluated up to the 6th class. Spelling in other subjects is not evaluated at all. Additional technical aids, such as a laptop, may be used to help the child. In fact, a laptop offers an excellent option to compensate dyslexia, but more about this later.

As of the 7th class, this rule can be extended to higher classes for individual pupils at the discretion of the school. Therefore, whether and to what extent a child receives help from his or her school depends on the persuasiveness of its parents. Stubbornness is recommended here if the child is not reading and spelling as it should be and a further deterioration is to be feared. It's worth the effort.

In so-called borderline cases, which can become very serious very quickly, it is also advisable to take advantage of the equilibrium of advantage and, even if faced with an initial rejection, to remain stubborn and demand your rights. Parents should not be afraid to take advantage of advice, protection and help for their child. They should not expect the school to approach and advise them on how their child can conquer its chronic dyslexia. Parents must be proactive.

The positive side of this new change in education is that children with dyslexia have a better chance than before of gaining a good school-leaving qualification. This strengthens the self-confidence and enhances their prospects of success.

Personally speaking, I think it is a good thing that this protection has now been extended to these children. Countless children who were forced in the past to write one unpractised dictation after another over years considered this to be little better than a humiliating running of the gauntlet that was graded. It is right that dyslexia sufferers are no longer branded as stupid. And it is simply wonderful if they manage to achieve their school-leaving certificate or even the *Abitur*!

On the other hand, a high price must be paid for these improvements. If the evaluation of spelling is diminished, it is to be feared that, overall, German as a subject will also be downgraded. This is playing with fire.

Long-term consequences

Frankly, I find the state's treatment of "dyslexics" very worrying, as the goal of ensuring that all children can read and spell *competently* is silently discarded. The reality is that for one in five children the school fails to achieve this goal. Far from conquering dyslexia, this approach only ensures that it accompanies the victim into adulthood.

A further downside of this dilemma is that the dyslexia "wounded" who do not manage to master their problem live the rest of their lives in the fear of being exposed. This may become evident at the workplace when there is a need to read a lot of information quickly, sometimes in a foreign language. Or in the early throes of romance where, on falling in love, the dyslexia sufferer yearns to express his or her feelings in writing. Or in the family if the person wishes to help his or her children do their homework. But the main challenge comes where one wishes to further one's education and enrich one's learning with the knowledge of this world. Anybody who can only read laboriously is at a decided disadvantage. The temptation to give up reading books altogether is almost irresistible.

Overall, it would seem that increasingly fewer people are in the habit of reading as adults. Could there be a connection with the fact that schools increasingly avoid addressing the subject of dyslexia? I cannot prove this. I suspect this may be a factor, but also that in this present epoch children are now developing more slowly.

If schools cannot effectively teach children to read and write, it is obvious that parents need to do something themselves about this situation. And many do this, practising regularly with their children and, additionally, trying to help them through extra tuition or private therapies. Extra tuition is often the poorest choice, as it usually only involves the lacklustre repetition of that which the child is already unable to do: read and spell.

Therapies, on the other hand, often similar to remedial courses in schools – are more intensive and individual. Professional providers first compile a 'needs profile' of the individual schoolchild, and this profile is used to design a course for the child with special exercises ranging from letters of the alphabet to grammatical exercises. This methodological-didactic approach frequently requires the child to attend lessons twice a week. Some institutes insist that parents sign an annual contract with a monthly fee of €250. Despite this, the results are repeatedly disappointing when taken as a whole. In most cases the success achieved is modest when compared to the outlay and effort. Better results are almost always achieved if schoolchildren practise with a PC or the actual letters of the alphabet.

> Schools and the majority of therapies cannot help children to master reading and spelling. The schools have too little time and inadequate personnel for this purpose, and both schools and therapies often fail because they do not employ reliable methods which achieve measurable improvements within a specific time-period. In other words: therapy and school cannot teach your child to read and spell competently.

2.   A single brain region and a heap of letters
The true cause of dyslexia – and the only effective solution

"I simply don't believe it! The average mark of our pupils in unpractised dictation is somewhere between 4.5 and 5! Look, here it is in black and white, I've evaluated the marks for this school year." I pushed the documents into the middle of the table.

Four of us were sitting together in the *Kennedy Tutorial School* in Tuttlingen, Southern Germany, evaluating the children's progress in German. It was a frosty November morning in 1991. My three colleagues, Sabine Maler, Anita Pankler and Thomas Detmold, leaned over to examine my written assessment. Trouble appeared to be brewing in the room, and the meeting was nowhere near over.

Frau Maler leaned back slowly and stared at the edge of the table. "I've worked for thirty-five years in primary schools but I've never seen anything like this!" With pursed lips, she looked at me with an expression of anticipation. "What now?"

Before I could answer, Herr Detmold interrupted with dismay. "I know with absolute certainty that Dennis Scherer got a 1 two weeks ago in his last German test! And now he has a 5! Something has to be wrong here! "

Frau Maler looked at him in surprise. "A 1.0! What kind of test was it?"

"A difficult grammar test, the class average was 3.4. Dennis was the best."

Frau Maler shoved the papers forcefully across the table where they landed directly under the critical gaze of Herr Detmold. "And why has he a straight 5 in dictation? After all, we've practised so much with him. It just doesn't add up!"

She sighed and drew a deep breath. "You're right, Herr Detmold," she said quietly. "From time to time, the children's performance can really astonish you, but the very next day you think they're worse than first-year pupils. The devil only knows what's going on here."

Herr Detmold did not reply, but studied the documents with a serious expression. At this moment, Frau Pankler, an experienced and caring German teacher originally from the former GDR, interjected.

"We can practise with the children as much as we want, but they're spelling simply refuses to improve!" Frustrated, she laid her notepad on the table.

Herr Detmold looked up from the documents, shaking his head. "I'm afraid you're right. If I understand this column correctly, Dennis has actually deteriorated in dictation from a 4 to 5. He's making an average of eight spelling mistakes more today than a year ago!"

Frau Pankler glanced over her shoulder at him. "You've read it correctly – unfortunately! To be honest, this is exactly what I've been worrying about." She then turned to me, speaking her mind freely.

"You know, Mr Kennedy, the children are still gripped with fear when it comes to class tests. I don't mean nervous jitters. I'm talking about existential fear. They feel as if they're running the gauntlet when it comes to dictation, time and time again."

"Yes, it's absolutely awful," interrupted Frau Maler. "Some of them wake up during the night before unpractised dictation and can't get back to sleep. I know that Julia Vogler has even begun to sleepwalk."

Herr Detmold nodded in agreement. "Recently, Frau Braun told me that Anton had to vomit again right after breakfast before the last dictation. To be honest, it's not the first time I've heard this."

"I'm continually telling the children that they've nothing to be afraid of," added Frau Maler. "But it doesn't really help. Tina Riess' mother doesn't know what she should do, because her little girl keeps saying she doesn't want to go on living."

However, Herr Detmold, a valiant soul, refused to throw in the towel yet. "Maybe we should send the children to a psychologist." The atmosphere was deteriorating even further and, apart from growing frustration, the discussion was leading nowhere.

"Okay people," I interrupted. "Time out! I'd like to adjourn our meeting, as we're not making any further progress. To sum up: We realised a year ago that practising dictation and spelling with our pupils in groups of five was not achieving the desired results. Therefore, we formed smaller groups with a maximum of three pupils who then came to German tuition twice a week for 90 minutes. Most importantly, we endeavoured to improve our didactic, methodical approach. Well, the results could be better. I'm just as disappointed as you!"

I nodded to my colleagues. "Thank you very much for your commitment and dedication, but we've covered enough ground for today, and we could all more than do with a break. Let's wrap it up for now."

Method Spaghetti

As my three colleagues slowly left the room, I began to ponder. Where do we go from here? What should we do now? For the first time in my career as an educationalist, I was completely at a loss.

The numerous scholastic measures we had implemented in the past year to improve the pupils' results in German began to flash before my eyes as if in a film. We had come to notice that the children who came to us for extra tuition in German simply seemed to forget how a word should be written and read correctly. Put another way, the information was failing to make the transition from the short-term to long-term memory. We therefore examined the recommendations of leading memory specialists and came across the highly successful system developed by Sebastian Leitner, a spaced repetition method employing *flashcards*.

Cards on which words are written are contained in boxes in different compartments. A word is written on a card and learnt, and this is then filed in the first compartment. The child should know on the next day how the word is written, and be able to read it properly. When they have achieved this, the card is moved to the next compartment towards the back of the box. However, it is replaced in the first compartment if the child makes a mistake. The box contains a total of five compartments, and the objective is to ultimately have all the cards in the fifth. Each word and its correct spelling will by then also have made the transition from the child's short-term to long-term memory.

This method appeared comprehensible and transparent to us, so we decided to employ it. Conscientiously. Month after month. Despite this, the hopes we invested in this system were only matched by the disappointing results – not one single child improved their spelling or reading in German. Dictation was still more than unsatisfactory.

Luckily enough, another promising approach also existed. Insights gained in *remedial education and occupational therapy* indicate that children achieve better results when they combine learning and motion. When it comes to spelling, this means "dictation in motion". We didn't waste any time. We soon had pupils flitting from one place to another. They read parts of their dictation in one corner of the room, while their desk was in the other corner where they wrote down the text they had just read. Parents then repeated the dictation with their children at home in the usual manner.

We had finally found a strategy that achieved success! Many children even improved their marks and got a 1. However, the completely frustrating aspect of this approach was our failure to repeat these successes in unpractised dictation. Marks achieved were, in the main, between 4 and 5 again, and a 6 was nothing unusual.

These efforts gradually led us to realise that we would not progress any further through memorising and intensive learning alone. But what should we do? We had already tried the entire spectrum of methods known to German specialists and educators. By degrees, we began to feel like the doctor who bombards his patients with tablets – and still fails to achieve any improvement. Was the diagnosis wrong?

And then the penny dropped! A single question began to occupy our thoughts. What if these children were dyslexic – and not just one or two, but all of them? This seemed highly improbable. We were a completely normal tutorial school trying to help perfectly normal pupils. But if all these children were dyslexic, it would be wrong for us to continue with the usual spelling exercises. Instead, we would need to employ special methods which were also used in institutes that work with pupils experiencing difficulties in reading, writing and arithmetic (dyslexia and dyscalculia). Our analysis of the situation indicated that we would have to go back even further, using the *synthetic method* to get right to the start of the reading and writing learning process.

This logical approach starts with basic training involving the letters of the alphabet, the maxim being *phonetic* pronunciation (that is, b and not "bee", t not "tee"). Straight away, and much to our surprise, the children showed positive results, even though the method is anything but playful...

The next steps, based on the findings of educational psychologist Heide Buschmann, saw them progress from letters to syllables, then from syllables to the complete word. This also works inversely, thanks to hyphenation. Words are broken up into smaller components: syl-la-ble, words, dic–ta–tion. We also incorporated motion into these exercises again, with the children clapping while they pronounced the syllables, or they emphasised these by swinging their arms. This was obviously a lot more fun than spelling, but we scored no successes with regard to spelling skills.

Although this technique is still regarded by leading specialists and institutes in the treatment of difficulties in reading, writing as *the* method for improving reading and writing skills, not one child in our school showed any signs of improvement. Dictation remained sheer agony for the children, parents and teachers. Good grades in dictation counted!

The consequence for us was a greater appreciation of the need to structure our work in an even more individual manner. The majority of learning specialists believe each child should develop its own strategy to master its problems regarding reading and spelling. And, in point of fact, not all of them shared the same difficulties. For example, Mike scored a particularly high number of errors when it came to upper- and lower-case letters, word extensions and duplications. Then again, Janine had difficulties in placing letters in the right sequence, mixed up letters and frequently started a sentence with a lower-case letter. We therefore identified the weak points for each child and developed an individual educational plan for each pupil and, where the teachers focused together with the children on the tricky areas, things actually improved in most cases! Unfortunately, the pupils continued to make a lot of mistakes in other respects. It was enough to drive you mad with exasperation!

While we were involved in these efforts, we also introduced individual motivation training based on the *Leger method* much praised by specialists. Put simply, each child is encouraged to read more. The fundamental assumption of this method is that pupils who do not want to read refrain from doing so because they don't want to, not because they have difficulty. They fail to perceive the added value in this exercise because they do not realise that it could help them more than playing computer games or watching films. We explained to the children in their uncertainty that they would run less of a risk of getting poor marks and being rejected by their peers and teachers, if they read more. We told the more daring among them that they would be more successful and gain greater recognition through regular reading.

It was not only the children who embraced this method. Their parents were also won over rapidly to this approach, which was not really surprising as this was why they had come to seek our help in the *Kennedy Tutorial School*! We also encouraged the children to pick up a book instead of watching television through a reading competition with lots of attractive prizes. The intention was to run the project for a year, a generous time frame, but hardly any child showed any *voluntary* interest in picking up a book at the end of this period. Even worse, the children started to simply give up. "What's the point of all this! ", they seemed to think and, instead of reading a book, they at best only looked at comics or continued watching television.

It appeared that all our best efforts had been in vain. We hadn't scored any breakthroughs. We hadn't even been able to prevent some of the children becoming ill as a direct result of their attendance at the school.

I was on the verge of despair, wondering how on earth we were supposed to continue. Was the solution to be found somewhere else entirely? The fact was that nearly all our pupils were lacking in focus and had difficulties concentrating. They were easily distracted, unsettled and/or "dreamy". I came to the conclusion that a child that is unable to concentrate can hardly be expected to perform well in reading and writing, so I decided to try a neurological approach.

Neuropsychologist and child psychiatrist Dr Fritz Held had been involved in researching the area of poor concentration for many years. He demonstrated that targeted stimulation of the brain can improve the release of the neurotransmitters dopamine and serotonin which, in turn, leads to enhanced concentration. As a consequence of these findings, we commenced a trial aimed at improving the attentiveness of children with the aid of concentration training and relaxation exercises at the beginning and end of German tuition. We even used special accompanying music in part during these endeavours.

The newly introduced exercises soon achieved positive results, as the children were without a doubt quieter and more even-tempered than previously. However, this did not last long when they were handed back their unpractised dictation, as their efforts were covered in corrections penned in red. The average mark was 5 or 6 and, in most cases, their dictation bore the simple advice of the teacher: "You've got to practise more!"

In other words, the poor performance of our pupils in spelling was not solely due to a lack of concentration. Clear evidence of this was reflected in the fact that some of these pupils frequently achieved good results in other subjects. We then focused on training grammar, as we suspected that the children had possibly failed to grasp the rules of grammar correctly. And, lo and behold, as it seemed in our meeting, Herr Detmold had hit the nail on the head. Many of the children achieved better marks in grammar exercises!

However, none of them seemed to read a book with any frequency, and they all continued to perform poorly in spelling.

Finally, I consulted with my teaching staff to see if the problem could be traced back to the teaching material used. We improved German tuition by introducing superior material: syllable memory and tile-based word games, tutor systems (LÜK), crossword puzzles, board games and a multitude of individual and colourful exercise sheets. We also continued our regular contact with parents to ensure that our methods were applied at home in a purposeful manner. We did everything we possibly could and would have moved mountains, just to keep the children on board and help them further. Despite this, at the end of a year of trials and testing, the results of our efforts were as clear as night and day – not a single pupil had improved his or her spelling skills or had become a voluntary, competent reader through our German tuition. On the contrary, some of them were even worse than before!

The methods which we had employed were used everywhere, if not in all tutorial schools, then with absolute certainty in dyslexia institutes. They were the latest – and best – methods education had to offer to improve reading and spelling ability. We were using *state-of-the-art* techniques, but despite all our efforts, we had failed to progress one single step in dictation.

I asked a pupil who had practised for an entire year with us a simple question: "Thomas, is the word "table" written with a *capital* T or a *small* t?" (Nouns in German are written with a capital letter).

"With a capital T," he replied without hesitation.

"Why's that, Thomas?"

"Because it's a noun!"

"Then why do you nearly always write it with a small t?"

"I don't know," said Thomas, with a look of uncertainty on his little face.

And, I thought, neither do I! What could be the problem? Why had all our best efforts borne no fruit? Either the methods were bad, or these reading and writing difficulties were simply insurmountable. Either we hadn't the right means to tackle the problem, or these children were incurably uneducable.

I simply felt there must be a solution to this problem. But never in my wildest dreams could I have expected that solution to be so obvious, so simple and so effective...

30 mistakes with an IQ of 120

Frau Schmidt and I were waiting patiently in the practice of Dr Fritz Held, child psychiatrist and specialist for dyslexia. Furnished in an old-fashioned but welcoming style and decorated with children's pictures, the waiting room was empty. Nobody had come in in the last 30 minutes. That's just fine, I thought. He'd have all the time in the world to conduct all the necessary tests with Sandra, Frau Schmidt's daughter. Both Frau Schmidt and I were completely baffled at this stage, as Sandra never read books and was making more than 30 errors regularly in her dictation, even though she was practising on a daily basis. While we were racking our brains and wondering if taking this step would finally change anything, the door suddenly opened.

"Please come in, Frau Schmidt. And you too, Herr Kennedy." We followed his assistant as she ushered us into Dr Held's consulting room. "Please take a seat," said Dr Held.

An impressive man, I thought. Tall and slim, Dr Held spoke to us quietly in a measured tone. "The results of the *Hamburg Wechsler **Intelligence Test*** and *Nonverbal Intelligence Test for Children* from Snijders-Oomen indicate an intelligence quotient (IQ) of 122."

"Is that good or bad?" interrupted Frau Schmidt.

"That's not just good ... it's very good indeed!" said Held, calming her fears. "Your daughter should be attending *Gymnasium* (advanced secondary school) and not the *Hauptschule* (lower secondary school)."

"I knew it!" exclaimed Frau Schmidt. "Sandra was always a lovely child, so it's no surprise that she's a bright spark too! She deserves better, and shouldn't end up doing temporary jobs like I do."

I'd known Frau Schmidt for some time, but this was the first occasion I'd seen an expression of such relief on her pale, weary and, quite frankly, exhausted face. And it came as no surprise, because the threat of having to repeat a year was hanging over Sandra. This was the first result in a long time that led us to believe that she wasn't a completely hopeless case.

"What does the *Nonverbal Intelligence Test* involve? "I asked Dr Held.

"It doesn't include reading and writing. Sandra has her problems in these areas, but the ability to read and write is not contingent on her intelligence."

"Do you mean I'm not stupid?" interrupted Sandra.

"No Sandra, I can safely say that you are in no way stupid," replied Dr Held, smiling pleasantly at her. He then turned to me, saying, "Herr Kennedy, you have to understand that these children are both blind and deaf when it comes to *letters*."

"You mean they all suffer from impaired sight and hearing?" I asked, ironically.

"No, that's not what I mean. Visual and hearing capabilities do, of course, need to be tested as well. But the reason for dyslexia lies at another brain level, the reading and writing centre. This is where letters are stored and called up as raw material during reading and writing. The findings are obvious. This procedure can only be successful if this region has *matured*! And this state of maturity has not been achieved in Sandra's case and that of all other dyslexics."

"You mean Sandra's case involves dyslexia *and* a retardation of maturity?" I inquired in astonishment.

"Yes, it's one and the same thing. Or, to be more precise, it's a case of a specific learning disability in the reading and writing function. The ability to read and write should be understood as a stage of child development. It's a biological phenomenon."

"I see ...," I replied, somewhat confused. "But what exactly are you trying to tell us?"

"Well, the ability to read and write depends on the level of progress of a child's development. And I'm not just talking about its intellectual potential. I especially mean the *biological* development of these functions. A child first learns to walk upright, and it usually masters this in its first year of life. It starts to learn to speak at the age of about two. From the age of three onwards, it gradually loosens its bonds with the mother – a well-known phase of defiance. At the same time, it learns to play with others, and it gradually begins to follow the rules of games. The ability to read and write is nothing more than another stage in the child's development, in exactly the same way as walking, speaking, severing the bonds with the mother or getting on with others are."

As I endeavoured to digest this point of view, Dr Held turned to Frau Schmidt. "Frau Schmidt, you have to ensure that Sandra memorises the letters of the alphabet, absorbing them firmly and very, very deeply until she has overcome her difficulties in reading and writing. And it's quite simple to do this. Sandra needs to type text on a typewriter every day, 20 minutes a day. And she has to keep this up until the spelling errors disappear and she can read well."

"But she's not able to type with all 10 fingers," said Frau Schmidt with concern.

"That doesn't matter, she doesn't have to," replied Dr Held reassuringly. "Sandra, I want you to type with just one finger, the one you hold your pen with. Do you understand?" "Yes, we do," replied Sandra's mother cheerfully.

"Okay, we'll get to grips with this problem together!" Dr Held made a note, then turned to me again. "Herr Kennedy, what are your results in German like in your tutorial school?"

I drew a deep breath. "Do you want an honest answer?" He looked into my eyes, and I heard myself mutter a single word: "Poor."

"I'm not surprised," he answered dryly. "These children need *letters*, not words. They need to absorb letters through their senses, through seeing, hearing and touching, through a curative approach. They need to continue this until the region of the brain responsible for reading and writing has matured. Ah, but just listen to me! Sorry, I tend to go on a bit too much. If you like, I can let you have a few documents containing the findings of my thirty years of research."

"I'd be delighted, Dr Held," I answered in surprise, thinking to myself that it couldn't hurt to read these.

However, my doubts started to grow on the long journey home with the Schmidt family. 20 minutes of typing a day? That's supposed to solve Sandra's problems in German? Just this repetitive task on a typewriter? That's a pretty old-fashioned method! No wonder his practice is empty...

A hot lead

Memorising letters to help specific brain maturation? Well, I'd never heard of this method, but the mostly widely talked about techniques which were part of the conventional cannon had all failed to help our pupils. And apart from this, the hypothesis that reading and writing skills should be regarded as a stage of child development fascinated me. Not solely because, on further reflection from a scientific point of view, it was so obvious and I asked myself why nobody had come up with it much earlier, but also because it was a completely new approach to the problem; one that gave me hope.

I gave up all thoughts of enjoying a relaxing weekend following the visit to Dr Held, burying myself instead in his treatises. These included many special editions of the *Der Kinderarzt*, a professional journal addressing paediatrics, and I was struck after only a few pages by the superior, above-average quality of the contents. I also increasingly noted that Dr Held was in no way alone in his perception. His theory that the ability to read and write represented a further stage in the cultural evolution of mankind was supported by the findings of research conducted by three leading scientists who had studied the phylogenetic development of human thought processes intensively for many years.

Konrad Lorenz, Director of the Max Planck Institute for Behavioural Physiology and a Nobel Prize laureate in medicine (1973), had demonstrated the existence of sensitive phases of imprinting during the development of animals and humans. Lorenz had imprinted himself on young geese following hatching by imitating their mother. He was the first living being that the little goslings took notice of, and as they grew up, the geese followed him everywhere, even paddling after him in the lake! Nature had therefore ensured that after hatching the first living being in its immediate vicinity imprinted itself on the gosling, which it then regarded it as its "mother".

These sensitive phases are an innate feature of all living creatures, serving the automatic adoption or, to put it more clearly, the memorising of important information mirrored from the immediate environment. Furthermore, we humans are imbued with inherent programs which are executed in a completely involuntary manner. For example, we do not need to actively think of the rules of circulation and body temperature. Lorenz described these as closed programs, postulating further that we possess other programs in areas of behaviour which ensure our survival. Programs such as aggression and flight are triggered automatically in the event of a threat. Only our mind and ability to think enables us to steer our behaviour in *another* direction.

Programs are therefore the primary controllers of our behaviour. But reading and writing are cultural achievements which have to be learnt. Where was the connection in this context?

According to Irenäus Eibl-Eibesfeldt, Professor for Zoology and Head of the Research Department for Human Ethology at the Max Planck Society in Seewiesen, Bavaria, these two things are completely compatible. He illustrated how *blind* children laugh through a series of photos. Ah! This was unequivocal evidence that laughing is an innate behavioural pattern! He revealed further how human beings demonstrate certain behavioural patterns at a highly developed cultural level all over the world. "Among primitive peoples, powerful chieftains who visit another tribe and perform a war dance are accompanied by a child who waves a green frond as a symbol of peaceful intentions. In our cultural circles, the host impresses with military pomp, while the state visitor is also presented with a bouquet of flowers – usually presented by a young girl," noted Professor Eibl-Eibesfeldt. We have therefore learnt to modify our aggression and adapt it to suit the situation.

Lastly, and by no means least, Hoimar von Ditfurth, Professor for Psychiatry and Neurology, illustrated in his book on the evolution of human consciousness, *"Der Geist fiel nicht vom Himmel. Die Evolution unseres Bewusstseins"*, that our ability to think and learn is a result of evolution. In a work as gripping as a whodunit, von Ditfurth related the history of our brain and its development over thousands of years, where an extremely extended period was followed by the development of our brainstem, the part of our brain responsible for controlling our vegetative behaviour (including breathing, the regulation of blood levels and simple automatic reactions). The diencephalon (mid-brain) evolved subsequently after another long period, controlling the programs which govern aggression, flight and sexuality. This marked the birth of emotions.

Human beings were thus taking their first tentative steps on a journey of development, but would we survive? A further inconceivably long period saw the development of the telencephalon (cerebrum) which better ensured survival. According to von Ditfurth, it controls advanced cognitive abilities such as the planning of future activities and communication using language. It is also responsible for *learning* as we know it today: the acquisition of knowledge, ability and behaviour.

The works of these three authorities therefore proved that human beings have both innate and acquired behavioural patterns. Interestingly enough, human beings can only acquire new behavioural patterns if their biological development has progressed sufficiently. Dr Held's hypothesis therefore fitted seamlessly into the observations of these three scientists, as he ultimately regards the ability of human beings to read and write as nothing other than a further stage of cultural development.

According to Held, the ability to combine symbols and letters automatically is an innate skill. However, in common with speech, it is an *open* program. The brain of a child needs to be fed words if it is to acquire speech, and the child then constructs meaningful sentences intuitively through imitation. However, this entire process can only function if a vital prerequisite is fulfilled: the biological maturity of the brain's center of speech.

Dr Held assumed that the same phenomenon must be responsible for spelling. The center for reading and writing also needs to be fed letters if the child is to learn to read and write, obviously! This must continue until the child can automatically position the appropriate letters in the right sequence. Reading is the ability to identify a series of letters as a word - automatically. On the other hand, the prerequisite for this is the biological maturity of center of the brain which is responsible for reading and writing.

This all sounded very convincing to me, but it didn't take long for the first question to arise. If speaking, reading and writing are natural phenomena whose manifestation is merely related to biological maturity, how does immaturity in the brain occur? Why are children like Sandra affected, but others not?

I delved into Held's documents again and discovered a range of possible triggers which he had identified during his many years as a paediatrician:

- Factor number one: Heredity. Many parents of his young patients had told Dr Held that they themselves experienced problems with reading and writing during childhood. It occurred to me at this point that parents in the *Kennedy Tutorial School* had told me exactly the same thing! Gradually, a clearer picture began to develop ...

- Moreover, Dr Held had noticed that many children who experience an oxygen deficiency at birth suffer from dyslexia at a later stage. The same applied to premature births where the child's brain had not yet developed completely on leaving the womb. Cases like this were also evident among our acquaintances.

- Dr Held also noticed that a severe illness suffered as a baby or toddler can lead to slow maturity. This finding also fitted into the overall picture, because concerned parents had repeatedly told me during registration interviews of severe illnesses suffered by their children and asked me if these could be the cause of problems at school. Even though I had waived this aside at the time, I now thought that there could be something in it.

- Naturally enough, Dr Held postulated that *psychological* "brakes" to the maturing process could also be possible causes. For example, children who were neglected in their first three years and continually exposed to different attachment figures suffered more frequently from delayed maturity.

The subject of maturity just kept popping up! When an intelligent child is sent to school too soon, this can lead to reading and writing difficulties. The reading and writing center has simply not developed far enough *biologically* to absorb letters reliably. Sending these children to school earlier will not help improve this innate condition. They need to practise with letters all the more to stimulate maturation of the center for reading and writing.

However, the majority of schools have been employing "modern" methods for many years which, in the first class, dispense with the "mindless" learning of letters and opt instead for a holistic approach to reading and spelling where children very soon learn entire syllables and words (often before they have learnt the alphabet completely) and deduce the letters themselves from the context. Unfortunately, a method which sounds child-oriented is completely counterproductive for those children with a predisposition for dyslexia i.e. whose reading and writing center has not matured enough.

Conversely: If the "borderline" child *would not have* suffered from reading and writing difficulties by learning the alphabetic method exclusively, it was bound to suffer from dyslexia where *this* method was employed! In other words, the school can contribute to reading and writing difficulties. The "whole-word" and "syllable" methods poses no difficulty for a child with a mature reading and writing centre, as it can pick out individual letters from syllables and words and imprint these effectively. However, in the case of a child with an immature or *borderline immature* reading and writing centre, the method can even intensify this deficit.

(The best example of the futility of an alternative methodology that ignores the fundamentals of learning is the 'Reading through Writing Method' by Jürgen Reichen. The children were allowed to write as they wished without correction, thus imprinting themselves repeatedly incorrectly. After much controversy and with little success, this method has thankfully fallen into disuse).

It was suddenly clear to me why so many children who came to us had previously exhibited a continually deteriorating school performance as the demands on their reading and spelling abilities relentlessly increased. The names of numerous pupils who had endured this journey shot through my head. "Doctor Held, you've hit the nail on the head!" I thought aloud to myself as I placed his material to one side.

I grabbed a pen and paper and began to summarise these findings for our work. Furthermore, I also noted that reading and spelling difficulties can present themselves as a singular problem or in combination with one or more other developmental delays. Dr Held frequently observed reading and writing difficulties in combination with delayed speech development. Further combinations such as immaturity in fine and gross motor skills, numeracy and attentiveness were also encountered with the same frequency. That's it! It all fitted perfectly! Stefanie, Robert, Annemarie, Martin, Zina ..., and whatever the others' names were ... at least ninety per cent of our pupils fell into one of these categories, and sometimes even into several. If I was honest with myself, I could hardly think of one who didn't fit at least one of these criteria. How astonishing!

But hang on, if Held was right, it meant that practically everything we had tried up until now had been wrong. And the same applied to all other tutoring institutions and dyslexia centres! But was this really possible? Could every method currently employed to combat dyslexia be based on a fallacy, purely through the failure to appreciate this insight? Could it be that the entire professional community involved in the treatment of dyslexia had backed the wrong horse? After all, we weren't the only ones achieving poor results. *Every* school was in the same boat, regardless of whether they were special needs or secondary level schools, and this was reflected right across the country.

There was only one way to find out if Dr Held's hypothesis was correct: analyse it in detail and *put it to the test under practical conditions*. If the problem was really caused by immaturity in the regions of the brain responsible for reading and writing, and this could be overcome by regular alphabetic training in the manner put forward by Dr Held, then even pupils who had failed to respond to all previous efforts would finally make progress using the new method. If they only *imprinted* letters through all the relevant senses, namely sight, hearing and touch, then the relevant part of the brain could not help but mature and, ultimately, function correctly. It was obvious that the spelling and reading problem would eventually vanish completely! I wanted to see the results for myself, and set about trying it out.

"Come in please, Frau Beck" As with every visit, Anton's mother also took a seat at the table.

"Herr Kennedy, I'm sorry to disturb you, but I wanted to show you Anton's last dictation," she said in her usual friendly manner.

"No problem, I'd be delighted," I answered. To be honest, the prospect didn't exactly fill me with joy. Anton, who was in the eighth class in *Gymnasium (advanced secondary school)*, had come to our school 14 months ago with an average of 21 errors. He'd managed a 6.0 again four weeks ago, this time with 23 errors. Frau Beck had come to see us in recent months after almost every spelling test, complaining that things simply could not go on like this. She wanted to see results. I mean, why else would she send her child to the *Kennedy Tutorial School*?

My explanations and assurances that Anton's reading and writing skills had not yet "matured" and that this process took time had calmed her worries in the beginning. However, as she noticed after a few months that no improvement whatsoever had been achieved and Anton was still making between 18 and 24 errors, she now informed me that Anton would only be able to come to tuition once a week from now on, due to the new schedule. Not the best basis for future cooperation.

And here she was again, sitting in the usual place. What revelations did she have in store for me today? That she was going to take Anton out of the *Kennedy Tutorial School*? That he should give up this endless practising? Frau Beck placed the large dictation exercise book in front of me and opened the latest page. Her voice was unusually calm and quiet as she spoke.

"Herr Kennedy, look at this, he got a 1.0, not one single mistake! And his reading is also gradually improving...."

The breakthrough

A year of alphabet games and regular training with supplementary typing had paid off! And Anton wasn't alone – other children had also shown progress. The results were there to see in black and white, and I still found it hard to believe, especially in the case of some of the children, an improvement had seemed practically inconceivable. Convincing parents that practising with letters paid off took a lot of effort, especially as the progress achieved over many weeks appeared to be very little. But it was precisely the long duration of the process that substantiated Dr Held's hypothesis.

Seeing and feeling letters coupled with their relevant phonetic sounds transmits impulses via the sensory centres to the regions of the brain involved in reading and writing. On arrival, these impulses cause the relevant synapses to "fire" thus stimulating cell growth, and the underdeveloped reading and writing center network grows and matures as genetically "intended". Cell growth continues, but the ability to read and write does not always improve in proportion to this. The brain needs to reach a particular level of development to be able to combine letters correctly and identify series of letters automatically. As soon as the brain has reached the required level of maturity, your child is capable of achieving extreme progress sometimes practically overnight, an improvement which in itself is astonishing!

Dr Held had already hinted at this phenomenon while he was examining Sandra. He had gazed seriously into her eyes and given her a single tip: "Don't give up, even if you can't see any change at first". I have no doubt that Dr Held knew at this moment beyond a doubt that the maturing of the brain takes at least *one* year.

Anton was by no means the first child to show such clear progress during the breakthrough. Sudden improvements in marks were nothing unusual during these turbulent months, as our results table indicated. After three months of games with letters, 67 per cent of the pupils had improved on average by 1.5 marks in unpractised dictation. The figure was 72 per cent after 6 months, with pupils registering an improvement of about two marks. 93 per cent were achieving an improvement of three marks after 12 months. Seven per cent of pupils had, as in Anton's case, demonstrated no improvement whatsoever until the day on which everything changed. Luckily for Sandra, things moved even quicker, and she achieved an astonishing improvement of three marks within three months.

In the case of *reading*, perhaps the harder nut to crack, the results were also striking. After about 12 months, 87 per cent of parents at our school reported an improvement in their child's reading and willingness on their part to read books voluntarily.

After a year of stumbling around in the proverbial fog, followed by another year of games with letters and training through typing, there was no doubt any more on my part: The thesis relating to the maturing of reading and writing abilities was valid!

The true cause of dyslexia is neither to be found in the pupils' intelligence nor in their behaviour, but solely in the immaturity of the relevant brain region. And the system employed in our school and methods commonly applied to teach these children reading and spelling had only succeeded in making this immaturity worse.

3. "Is my child really dyslexic?"

How to identify dyslexia reliably

"What's the problem? Samantha's always been very good in German up until now. That last test was an exception, she just wasn't concentrating. Oh, you don't agree?" Frau Tischler looked anxiously at Herr Gruhl, her daughter's class teacher. He had invited her to this meeting to discuss Samantha's performance levels in German and English. He looked concerned.

"On the contrary, I've seen the enormous effort Samantha puts into her work. However, her last essay was much too short and full of spelling mistakes. And that was no exception. She even managed to get a 6 in her last dictation! It doesn't get much worse than that, I'm afraid"

"Yes, well, Herr Gruhl, but that dictation wasn't announced in advance, that's not fair, we couldn't practise it at home"

Remaining perfectly calm, Herr Gruhl explained that in *this* intermediate secondary school (*Realschule*) it was standard procedure to write unannounced and unpractised dictation. This was the only way to really test the child's writing skills. Samantha's spelling abilities were poor. And he knew from the English teacher that the girl continually made mistakes in vocabulary tests, even though her oral English was good.

"Which brings us to the reason for this meeting, Frau Tischler." Herr Gruhl drew a long breath and then said: "To be quite frank, I think Samantha may suffer from dyslexia. She has a learning disability."

"A disability? Sami? That's a load of nonsense! She's a very bright girl! You should see how good she is when she plays Memory! She was also good enough in primary school. She got a 3 in German. Why should she suddenly have a disability?" Extremely agitated, Frau Tischler then left and drove back home. She practically ran a red light twice on the way, braking each time at the very last moment. All she could think about was her Samantha. While reading to her daughter that evening, Frau Gruhl suddenly pressed the book into the girl's hand. "Why don't *you* read for a while!"

The mother noticed for the first time how hesitantly the girl read. Shouldn't that be much better in the fifth class? But then again, she can't have practised very much. She simply never picks up a book. Or could it be the other way around? Maybe Sami only reads so rarely because she finds it difficult?

Frau Tischler woke up repeatedly that night. She kept thinking about Herr Gruhl's suggestion to send Samantha to a remedial group for dyslexia. But wouldn't your child be branded as a result? Maybe her classmates would laugh at her. A learning disability – that sounds so awful! Frau Tischler tossed and turned in bed. Would it be better if they both continued practising together at home just as they had been doing before? The problem was, this did not seem to have got them very far – apart from her having to appear before Herr Gruhl! Was Sami really dyslexic? What in heaven's name should she do?

To be frank, Frau Tischler was lucky! Why? Because she had met a competent, sensitive and well-informed teacher who worked in a school that is academically professional in its approach. Lucky as well because this teacher had taken it upon himself to speak to her about the possibility that her daughter had dyslexia. Regardless of how shocking this news was for Frau Tischler, one thing was certain: her child was in good hands. Simultaneously, the school was trying to do something about her dyslexia.

Generally speaking, you should not expect the school to approach you if your child has difficulties with reading and spelling. Faced with this situation the majority of parents are left to their own devices. They see their child is struggling, and sometimes a relative or a friend may draw their attention to the child's difficulties and point out that they could be better. Parents then might ask themselves whether this could be dyslexia, or if the cause to these difficulties could lie elsewhere?

What then, are the warning signals to watch out for, the signs that draw one's attention to a possibility of dyslexia? Let's take a step-by-step look at the areas that give cause for concern.

Scenario 1:   Problems right from the outset

Frau Walter was appalled! Her six-year-old son Denis just forgot how to write the letter "d" – right before her eyes! He should have written it ten times. He made a good attempt at it at first, but every further letter was poorer and smaller. Denis only managed to scribble an "a" on the tenth attempt. It was almost as if Denis was writing the letters in sand, and these were then washed away when the tide came in. Every day, Frau Walter found herself starting right from the beginning again when she practised with Denis.

Right from the outset, the letters simply wouldn't sink in. Your child failed to identify them correctly and, consequently, was incapable of reproducing them properly. He also forgot them with alarming speed. It took an enormous effort on Denis's part to *paint* letters, and his writing of them showed every indication of tension. As time went on his difficulties increased. When writing the words were all close together, sometimes with gaps, sometimes without. Many letters were confused or inverted – for example:

"theweehls onthdusgoh rahnb audhraunb..."

"The wheels on the bus go round and round!"

Are you worried because your child has serious *beginner's* difficulties with writing? Are you concerned as to whether this will eventually later disappear of its own accord - or not?

Scenario 2: Problems arise with the first practised dictation

For Robert, a pupil in the fifth class at advanced secondary school (*Gymnasium*), the whole world was in disarray! His mother cried all day, and his father just sat in his TV armchair and ignored everybody. The reason: Robert had made 13 mistakes in German dictation and was given a 6 for his trouble. All the more surprising, as he always got a straight 1 in primary school! "Frau Rothe didn't give us any advanced notice of it. She just suddenly announced that we were going to write a dictation", Robert repeated constantly to his parents. "It's just not fair!"

Wasn't his spelling fine before? Step by step, together with him, his parents used to iron out all the child's mistakes in preparation for the next dictation. They also readily practised set given words, texts and vocabulary from the teacher, and your child had always received good marks as a result.

In Germany, unpractised dictation and unknown texts are often introduced at the start of the third or fourth school year or, as in Robert's case, on moving to secondary school – and suddenly your child starts to make many mistakes. This is often most evident at the end of dictation when time becomes short because your child is still busy correcting the first part. Does the sudden drop of up to three marks in English surprise you?

Scenario 3: German is fine, but the foreign language is a catastrophe

Heidi had just got a 4 in English. She was devastated! Particularly as all here friends had achieved better marks. After all, it was only yesterday evening that she had practised her vocabulary with her Mother, and she knew them all then! But now she had made a huge number of mistakes ... What was she going to say to Mother when she got home?

Are you disappointed by your child's results in vocabulary tests? Let's assume you have been practising vocabulary repeatedly with your child, and your child is able to spell them successfully – but not in school. Your child knows the vocabulary *orally*, but makes too many spelling mistakes. Does your child regularly write the endings of words in Spanish or French incorrectly, and is the conjugation of even simple verbs such as être, *avoir, parler* unreliable? Does the number of mistakes during *translations* into the foreign language increase markedly towards the end, yet your child simply doesn't understand why? Are you worried because your child has such unexpected difficulties in the first or second foreign language?

Scenario 4:   Your child reads poorly

Frau Schwarz and her son Freddie agreed that, every evening, Freddie would read two pages out loud from a Harry Potter book. However, whenever it slipped Frau Schwarz's mind, Freddie would not read anything, preferring to play with his Lego bricks. One evening, Freddie's sister Julia (who is two years younger) joined them, demanding that she should also have a chance to read. She took the book out of Freddie's hand and read clearly and with a very attractive intonation – fluently and far better than Freddie! Frau Schwarz was completely unsettled by this. She knew that Freddie was not a good reader for his age, but she never suspected he could be so far behind. Or was Julia just a high flyer, and Freddie was 'normal'?

Does your child have problems understanding unknown texts which are suitable for its reading age? Does your child like to read stories together with you, and do you notice that, with time, it can repeat complete passages and understand them? However, on reading a new text with the same vocabulary, your child makes very slow progress. On trying to identify unknown words with the aid of individual letters, your child has difficulty and tries to decipher the contents through *guesswork*. When it comes to English German and/or in foreign languages, your child reads texts imprecisely, replacing some words with make-believe words that more or less make sense. It blurs word endings in English or *foreign languages*. Above all: do you have a gnawing feeling of uncertainty, that something is wrong?

Scenario 5:   Your child used to read *better*

The book that Anna received from her grandmother for her birthday lay discarded far back under the bed; covered in dust. Frau Warnke found it while vacuuming and, completely stunned, stared at it in her hands. Why had Anna not tried to recover the book when it slipped down the side of the bed? She used to read voraciously. But then again, come to think of it, of late, Frau Warnke hadn't seen her daughter very often with a book in her hand. Anna preferred playing football with her new friends from the *Realschule (middle school)* secondary school. Was it normal for her to change her interests in this way, or was there something seriously amiss?

Do you feel unsettled because your child reads less than it used to? Does your child enjoy books less and less since secondary school has begun? Do they find the first foreign language difficult and the second one extremely so? Does this seem to be ruining any pleasure your child has with the language it otherwise may well enjoy speaking? Is your child now also increasingly experiencing, retrospectively, difficulties reading English texts, along with problems with English grammar and spelling?

Scenario 6:   Other subjects are also affected

Paul, third grade, is good at arithmetic, but he only got a 3 in the last test. His grandfather, who always helped him with his homework, was astonished. Paul failed to solve all three problems set, which had to be read. In fact, it looked very much as if he failed to understand any of the them.

Does your child make mistakes in arithmetic which you find hard to understand? Can your child count well, but has difficulties with tasks involving text? Or do they tend to read or write multi-digit numbers inversely (e.g., 12 instead of 21, or 756 instead of 657)? Your child can count correctly with these inverted numbers but, naturally enough, the answer at the end is wrong. Apart from this, does your child tend to confuse the arithmetic symbols +, −, x and ÷?

Oral performance in other subjects such as geography, biology or history can also be satisfactory. However, your child is at a loss as soon as it needs to gather information from books. If, for example, an essay is to be written on bees, the finished result is often much too short. Do you ask yourself whether your child simply does not like the subject in question, or whether its problems are related to their reading ability?

If even *one* of these conditions applies, you have good reason to be unsettled about your child's reading and/or spelling skills. They may well suffer from dyslexia. It is important to clarify this so that suitable measures can be taken at an early stage.

A large part of the uncertainty in this regard is due to the fact that dyslexia can arise in different forms. It may affect both reading AND spelling skills, or only one of the two. It can arise *immediately* when your child begins to learn to read and write. In this case, many parents try to compensate this deficit through learning by rote, that is by completely memorising the typeface and lettering sequence of individual words. This works only so long until your child needs to read and write *unpractised* words.

In addition to this, is the phenomenon of what I call 'late-stage' dyslexia which I addressed in the first chapter. Let us briefly regard the biology of this: the specific region of the brain that is responsible for the combination and sequencing of letters can deteriorate when it also has to deal with the first or second foreign language. The reason for this is that its borderline developed neural network could manage the lettering of the child's native language but becomes overwhelmed on the introduction of a first or second foreign language.

Late-stage dyslexia may be confined to only *one* language. However, my experience shows that, rather like woodworm, it usually pervades the reading writing skills in *all* languages: Spanish, French, and lastly English. This results in the young person making an increasing number of spelling mistakes in all three languages and, due to the added burden of reading difficulties, experiencing problems with grammar. A good reader who used to read a lot now seldom reads books, frequently with the excuse that they have no time for this because they have a lot to do for school. Thus, a most vicious circle is set up. Parents often attribute their child's apparent disinterest in books to being on the internet too often and or playing with friends.

Frequent misconceptions

In situations of this nature, *suppressing* the question of whether your child has dyslexia does not help. The best thing you can do is to obtain clarification about your child's condition. However, this is frequently not easy, as the question of how to recognise dyslexia *reliably* is hotly debated among specialists. Which is why I have compiled a list for you here of the most frequent *misconceptions* – meaning those characteristics which are most definitely *not* indications of dyslexia.

Misconception 1: Dyslexia can be identified by "typical mistakes"

Numerous researchers and teachers assume that typical mistakes exist which are indicative of dyslexia. For example, your child confuses letters (directional confusion) which look or sound the 'same,' d/b/ p/q, a/o, g/k, m/n, u/n, in addition, your child may reverse the *sequence* of letters or numbers. It may begin a sentence with a lower-case letter instead of a capital letter and often it simply fails to hear where short or long vowels are present in a word. It is almost as if your child were deaf and blind regarding letters.

In addition, if a child frequently masters *difficult* words but writes *simple* words incorrectly, this is also regarded as a sure sign of dyslexia. A child who *does not* make these types of errors is not regarded as dyslexic – even where they make extensive mistakes or reads poorly.

All I can say in this regard is that, yes, it is true that children with dyslexia *frequently* make the mistakes described above. There are also dyslexics who do not make these apparently "typical" mistakes, but do make normal spelling mistakes – unfortunately far too many!

By way of comparison, imagine you are travelling by car and need to stop because the rear left tyre is flat. The breakdown mechanic you call looks at the tyre and says to you: "There's no hole, and the valve is also okay. This tyre is not flat!" Then he drives off and leaves you alone on the side of the road. This is exactly what happens if the "dyslexia specialist" only examines and assesses whether damage has occurred *based on his own precise criteria*. Failing to find these, he decides there is no need for repair. I cannot describe how often parents describe this unfortunate procedure to me. Usually, dyslexia is not recognised – end of story.

Misconception 2: Dyslexia only exists if a child has difficulties in both reading and spelling

As soon as Tina (sixth class) came home from school, she'd grab the book she'd left on the breakfast table that morning and go to her room where she'd snuggle up into her "reading corner". Only later when Tina was hungry would her mother hear anything from her again. Everybody was baffled as to how Tina could write such imaginative essays and, simultaneously, make so many spelling mistakes – including most recently in English.

Sven (seventh class in *Gymnasium*) once again had enormous difficulties with his last essay. It just wasn't working out for him! He had really great ideas, but found it difficult to find the right words and expressions to get these across. And the result? He got a 4. He always needed to read the grammar rules in English and French twice or three times before he understood the content. He also had difficulties with texts in biology and geography. Sven's marks in other subjects became poorer and poorer, but he'd managed to 'keep up' through his oral performance. On the other hand, Sven always got a 1 or 2 when writing German and English dictation.

The fact is that it is possible to suffer from an isolated spelling disability and, conversely, an isolated difficulty in reading is also possible. They need not exhibit themselves together. However, if they occur *individually*, they are frequently not identified as dyslexia and, consequently, nothing is done about them. It is as if you demanded that your child first limp with *both* legs before any treatment can be considered.

Misconception 3: Dyslexia is *immediately* identifiable

In primary school, Janine now 5th class, *Realschule* achieved very good results in German, but all of that has changed. In her last English test, she made many, many mistakes. Her vocabulary was fine but, when it came to grammar questions, half of her answers were spelt incorrectly. In the dictation component, she had made a spelling mistake in practically every word. Overall, Janine has difficulties understanding the questions and texts. And, even more disturbing, Janine had been making more and more spelling mistakes in German. The times when she picks up a book have also become increasingly rare.

If your child had previously exhibited few or no problems with reading and writing, it is automatically assumed that its difficulties in foreign languages stem from a lack of talent in languages coupled with a lack of diligence. This is why extra tuition, participation in a school exchange or a spell at a language school in England, France or the USA are popular with parents here in Germany. These measures may lead to an improvement in spoken competence, but reading and spelling still remain poor.

Dyslexia can also occur in isolation in *one* language (and not be evident in other languages). Again, it may also occur as a late-stage condition when your child begins to learn foreign languages. Spoken language is one thing, the reading and writing of it another. That's straightforward enough is it not?

Misconception 4: Your child does not have dyslexia, but is simply lazy and unfocused

Frau Braun had a lot to hear from Hannes' class teacher this week. The pupil (third grade) was a disruptive influence, disturbing his classmates and continually making them laugh through his tomfoolery. On being challenged about this, he became cheeky and defiant. "If Hannes would stop being such a pain in the neck and concentrate on his work, he'd make fewer spelling mistakes", said Herr Baumann.

Children react differently to failure, depending on their character. Daredevils like Hannes react with defiance, aggression and rebellion, both at home and in school, and frequently clown about to gain the attention and recognition they so badly need.

Children who desperately seek security and acceptance within the class frequently react through tearfulness and ingratiation. They very often suffer from insomnia and nausea before they have to go to school. I occasionally hear from parents who say that their children ask why they should carry on living.

Many teachers unfortunately interpret these behavioural problems as the reason for and not the consequence of difficulties with reading and writing. Cause and effect are obviously muddled in this respect.

Misconception 5: A child that is weak in other subjects as well as German does not have dyslexia, but is simply not intelligent enough

For Sven, a fourth-grade pupil, life had not been easy of late. Everything in school was becoming increasingly difficult for him. Just this week, he had got a 4 in "Mankind and the Environment". He had tried to read the paper on "Birds in Winter and Summer" through several times, just like the teacher told him to, with moderate success. Herr Meister had written at the bottom of his test "Why did you not read chapter 4 and 5 CAREFULLY?" Perfect, just great! Thanks a lot, Herr Meister!

Then there was the mathematics test with three problems in text form to solve, which resulted in a measly four In Maths! a subject where he was usually good! Only the week before he received a 4.5 for his essay. He had tried to keep the essay *brief* because he always made so many spelling mistakes and, as he needed so much time to write, he could hardly develop his few ideas to put into it. His mother always said that, if he would only concentrate more, he would cope better, including in mathematics. Hmm, a lot of suggestions – but no results!

Sven's uncertainty increased and he felt that, no matter how hard he tried, he simply worsened. Why should he try so hard if he was only going to get bad marks and everybody around him only squeaked with annoyance (his mother) and complained long and loudly (his father) about him?

His mother had an appointment with Herr Meister to discuss the school's recommendation for her son. She returned home most upset. Later that evening, Sven heard his parents talking agitatedly in their bedroom. His mother's voice sounded strained as she said "A lower secondary school! That's what Herr Meister said. Sven's performance is bad in every subject, not just German. It's not just because of his poor reading and writing skills. He didn't say it directly, but it was clear he doesn't think that Sven is very bright."

Many teachers know today that dyslexia has nothing to do with intelligence. In spite of this, some teachers are convinced that supposedly dim children are academically weak across the board. And *the fact* that a child is not very bright exhibits itself in poor performance in numerous school subjects ... Given this, many teachers ignore *the fact* that the ability to read and write is of crucial importance in *every* subject if the content of texts is to be comprehended and ideas and thoughts are to be accurately reproduced in writing – free from fear of the dreaded red ink!

Intelligence tests frequently appear to confirm this misinterpretation – or at least where *unsuitable* tests are conducted. And that is still often the case today. Standard intelligence tests still examine areas in which your child is disadvantaged: reading, writing, arithmetic and verbal performance. In order to really estimate the intelligence of the child, only the quotient achieved in the *non-verbal* part counts, whereby reading and writing are excluded.

Do *you* know how a child with dyslexia is supposed to read a test of this nature correctly and answer it in writing? I don't – and those conducting the tests apparently have no idea either!

Misconception 6: The child's poor school performance is all down to conflicts in its family

"Micha, that's enough now! You've crossed out more than you've written correctly. Now sit down and copy the homework again. And stop fidgeting!"

On the recommendation of the class teacher, Frau Wagner had been checking her son's homework every day. Despite this, no improvement was yet noticeable. Frau Wagner was at her wits' end. So was Micha. "I'm sick and tired of this! I've already copied the damn homework twice!"

"But not properly, If you don't do it, you can forget about TV for the rest of the week!", his mother threatened.

"I hate you!" Micha ran out of the room and slammed the door behind him.

Just as every child reacts to failure according to their temperament, parents tend to do this too. They encourage, admonish or threaten your child to make them try harder, and this can lead to ferocious conflicts. Psychologically speaking, these conflicts are repeatedly cited as the cause of poor school performance. The dyslexia remains undetected and contributes to an ever worsening performance, thus demotivating the child. It is not unknown for teachers and the school management to condemn a family as dysfunctional and contend that nothing can be done to help.

On the other hand, many families react with indifference to poor school performance and, particularly where the mother and father were also poor pupils, it is regarded as normal. As a result, they do nothing to help their child, or they try to place the blame on the school. A conflict arises between the parents and teachers, with the child suffering even more as a result and feeling itself under increased pressure.

Repeatedly poor results only strengthen this momentum. According to child psychiatrist Dr Fritz Held, a vicious circle is created which spirals inexorably downwards. What was that about cause and effect?

Misconception 7: Your child simply has too little German

Shaking his head with exasperation, the teacher stared at Yüksel's most recent essay. Your child had an amazingly fertile imagination, but all these mistakes ... Well, it doesn't really come as a surprise, he thought. The child's mother hardly speaks German. That was evident at the last parent-teacher meeting. Where should the boy learn it? Handing back the essay to the fourth-grade pupil, he asked him. "Tell me, Yüksel, do you also speak German at home sometimes, or just Turkish?"

When dealing with the children of immigrants, it is easy to assume that poor spelling ability is the result of inadequate language skills. Your child then receives language development assistance, which is no bad thing in itself in cases where the child's knowledge of German could be better. However, this assistance is only of limited help if the child's problems are really due to dyslexia or if it has both language difficulties and dyslexia.

The most obvious explanation is not always the correct one.

When one considers the number of misconceptions disseminated in the internet and which, to a degree, are also common among teachers and even psychologists, it is no wonder that people become confused. It is very tempting to say "Yes, well, the teachers are probably right, my child doesn't have dyslexia at all!" But what if your child really is affected? They will only continue to suffer, and nobody will try to help your child.

For the youngster, dyslexia is a millstone around its neck. Reading and writing requires extreme effort, and the results achieved are frustrating. Poor spelling often leads to points being deducted for German essays and also for work in other subjects. Moreover, reading difficulties mean that your child finds it arduous to comprehend texts speedily in 'secondary subjects'. This applies equally to tasks involving text and the identification of numbers and characters in mathematics. In other words, *every* subject is affected. A sense of failure in school frequently leads to despondency which, in general, can have an overall negative impact on the child's schoolwork. Encouraged by parents, your child tries even harder – but without success! This in turn leads to sense of apathy and, much worse, hopelessness.

A pretty pass!

That is why it is so important to have a *reliable* method of determining whether your child has dyslexia or not. But how can that be possible when teachers – and even trained psychologists – are not always able to detect it?

Identifying dyslexia – in three steps

The method which I recommend you use here consists of three steps. Firstly, it is important to ascertain that your child does not have difficulties in reading and writing purely because their sight or hearing is poor. The second step involves a reliable method for determining whether your child has spelling difficulties. The third step enables you to detect a reading disability.

Step 1:   **Dyslexia, or impaired sight or hearing?**

Unimpaired vision is the absolute prerequisite for normal reading and writing. Contrary to the previously widespread assumption that impaired sight could also cause dyslexia, scientists now believe that visual reading disorders can *simulate* symptoms of dyslexia. This can usually be quite simply remedied by wearing spectacles.

Examinations involving 24,000 children have determined that every third child needs glasses. In order to be sure, I recommend that you consult an optician or ophthalmologist and have your child's vision tested.

Unimpaired binocular vision is an important prerequisite for optimum vision. As long ago as the mid-1950s, this awareness led Hans-Joachim Haase to think about new measuring techniques, making him a pioneer in the field of binocular full correction. Today, the methodology developed in this context is known as MKH (Measuring and Correcting Methodology after H.-J. Haase).

For further information about binocular full-correction see the Swiss website: **http://www.ivbs.org/information-in-english/**

Latent strabismus can be compensated for in mild cases by wearing special prism eyeglasses, while more severe cases can be helped through an operation on the eye muscle. Reading glasses or, in some cases, laser operating of the eye lenses help in the case of an accommodation disorder. Naturally enough, the advantages and disadvantages should be weighed up carefully prior to an eye operation. However, *if* it is the only measure which can possible ensure clear and unimpaired vision, it should seriously be considered.

Corrective measures to address eye problems may be enough to dispel any difficulties your child has with reading and writing. A probability, but not a certainty. Our experience has shown that dyslexia and visual impairments can indeed go hand in hand. For this reason, as soon as your child's defective vision has been ruled out or corrected through glasses, you should test your child for spelling and reading difficulties using the methods described below.

If you have any suspicion that your child has difficulty in hearing, have its hearing tested. Please note in this context that dyslexics with otherwise good hearing often *cannot differentiate between the phonetic sounds of letters.* These sounds do not register in the "immature" reading and writing area of the brain.

Step 2:   **Are spelling difficulties to blame?**

The solution is so simple that, initially, you probably will not believe it could be so simple. But, with 30 years of experience, I can assure you that it is. All children who were "diagnosed" as having spelling difficulties have profited immensely through using this method I'm about to describe. The result of highly targeted dyslexia training. They practised individual letters and, as a consequence, their marks in school improved significantly. So indeed, they were "dyslexics", otherwise they wouldn't have improved so significantly. The method employed is described below:

> The simplest way to detect a spelling disability is by the average number of mistakes your child makes in unpractised dictation or when writing essays. The more mistakes your child makes, the more pronounced the spelling difficulties are.

You should focus exclusively on *unpractised* dictation in this respect! *Practised* dictation is of little use as it can be learnt by heart. If your child does not write any unpractised spelling tests, you can check their spelling on the basis of their *essays* and see how many mistakes are made on average in other subjects. You could, of course, obtain a book of dictations or download some for its class level and try a few unpractised dictations with them.

Calculate the average number of mistakes in the last three unpractised dictations or essays to obtain an accurate assessment of spelling ability. Avoid assessing your child incorrectly based on one exception.

What is the average number of mistakes whereby you can accept that your child has spelling difficulties? In practice, you can adopt the following battle-tested guideline:

> If your child regularly makes an average of 10 mistakes in unpractised dictation, it has a spelling disability.

This guideline was developed by Dr Fritz Held, child psychiatrist and neurologist already mentioned previously in this book. We have employed it in the *Kennedy Tutorial School* since 1991 with great success.

This "borderline value" of 10 mistakes is valid for all classes and age-groups. The older the children become the more experience and knowledge they should have to manage the increasing length and complexity of the texts which they have to write from memory. With dyslexics, this is not so: they continue to make mistakes as they grow older and generally, the number of mistakes made, grows with them!

This provides important indications of the child's reading and writing skills (but *only unpractised* dictation *in the school* is authoritative!)

In addition to *the clear-cut* cases, let us examine borderline cases such as with Janine. A third-grade pupil, she makes no mistakes at all in *practised* dictation, and her handwriting is very attractive and easy to read. However, Janine makes considerably more blunders when it comes to *unpractised* dictation, averaging five or six mistakes. She most recently achieved a uniquely bad result of 11 mistakes. Janine is almost always gets a 2 for her essays, which is good. Curiously enough, in recent weeks, the number of spelling mistakes has increased steadily in her essays as well, even reaching 13 in the last composition.

And the explanation? Janine is, so to speak, a latent or potential dyslexic! You need to take such a case most seriously, as five mistakes in this setting respective dictation can rapidly become 20. It is also appropriate to consider those children who make few spelling mistakes, but make these *regularly*, and/or who dislike learning. It is better to treat *one to many* borderline cases of dyslexia than to neglect numerous children with reading and writing uncertainties. Recognizing the degree of immaturity of the reading and/or writing function, which varies from child to child, is crucial and improves with experience.

If your child regularly makes more than 10 mistakes in unpractised dictation or, although it makes *fewer* than 10, the number has recently increased, you should take appropriate measures *immediately*. Before you do this, first check the *reading skills* of your child on the basis of the tried and tested examples and criteria described below.

Step 3:   Does your child(also) have reading disability?

Maria had been literally battling her way through the story of the *'Fox and the Thieves'* for the last 15 minutes. Reading slowly, she continually overlooked letters and word endings, simply skipping these and even confusing entire words on three separate occasions. She stammered and stumbled her way through the sentences, completely wooden and without intonation. When her mother asked her what the story was about, your child was only able to give her a vague answer.

Frau Wichert had to practise reading with Maria because she would have never voluntarily picked up a book. If left on her own, Maria would spend the entire time watching television.

Frau Braun suspected that Philipp was affected by poor concentration. While learning biology together, Philipp continually copied words incorrectly from the biology book. Instead of *flower* he wrote *flowr*, for *earth*, erth and *world* became wrld.

Marc was, in fact, very good at reading and even picked up a book from time to time – but he would rarely read it to the end... If a book such as *Harry Potter* really seized his interest, he would read it through completely, even it took a lot of time and effort. However, he much preferred reading his Mickey Mouse comics, and these filled an entire shelf!

The characteristics that distinguish reading difficulties are as follows:

- An inability to identify mistakes

- Painstakingly trying to combine letters and syllables

- Confusing words which are written and spoken in a similar fashion (*here/hear/her, where/were/wear, your/you're, they/their/there*) and a failure to differentiate between similarly sounding verb forms (e.g. *meet/met, build/built*)

- Frequent confusion, overlooking or omission of critical endings in foreign languages e.g. in French il parl instead of *il parle; nus avon instead of nous avons*

- *Inaccurate* reading of texts or "reading" using make-believe words (instead of the correct ones) which are similar and fit into the text

- A repeated failure to understand the content

- And most significant: aversion/reluctance to reading

The main indication of reading difficulties is a reluctance to read and a preference for picture stories. If your child only *grudgingly* reads books composed mainly of text, but prefers comics or watches a lot of TV, this is not the cause of its reading difficulties, but most probably the consequence. However, if your child is not averse to reading, but exhibits several of the aforementioned characteristics, it is most likely also due to reading difficulties.

Your attention should also be piqued if your child is good at reading and understands texts – and still, on the whole, dislikes reading. It is possible that your child needs to expend a disproportionate amount of energy to read because the reading function of their brain is not operating fully automatically (that is the ability to recognise a sequence of letters effortlessly).

Anybody who learns to read, first imprints the letters individually in their brain center for letter sequencing and, over time, words impress themselves as a complete image. You have probably come across the following text in the internet or on a postcard:

> "Aoccdrnig to a rseearch taem at Cmabrigde Uinervtisy, it deosn't mttaer in waht oredr the ltteers in a wrod are, the olny iprmoatnt tihng is taht the frist and lsat ltteer be in the rghit pclae. The rset can be a taotl mses and you can sitll raed it wouthit a porbelm. Tihs is bcuseae the huamn mnid deos not raed ervey lteter by isltef, but the wrod as a wlohe."

This can be traced back to a doctoral thesis with the title *The significance of letter position in word recognition* written in 1976 by the psychologist Graham Ernest Rawlingson. He discovered that a *practised* reader no longer reads individual letters. He reads the first and last letter of a word, summarily recording the letters which should be contained in it, regardless of the sequence – and his brain then constructs the correct word from this jumble. This is why practised readers read much quicker than beginners. The reading function has been automated and no longer needs to be consciously controlled. If your child can only read slowly and with great effort, it is a clear sign that reading is not yet running on 'automatic'.

Conclusion

If these examples and criteria have helped you to determine whether your child has difficulties with reading and/or spelling, then you really have to act now! You have two options:

1. You can turn to the specialised teachers at your child's school and, using these distinguishing features, discuss remedial options with them.

   You should ensure that the rule, if appropriate, regarding *equalisation of advantage* is applied to your child, in order to protect them. You can also have a specialist conduct a dyslexic appraisal. However, be careful – even specialists are not always reliable when it comes to detecting dyslexia. In this case as always, your persistence is called for: try another specialist!

2. Continue reading this book and learn how to overcome dyslexia completely.

4.   Type your way to success!

How your child can improve by up to three marks – in dictation and essays, homework and foreign languages.

Her brows furrowed in concentration, Frau Straubinger combed through her weekly schedule – backwards and forwards, up and down

	Mon	Tues	Wed	Thurs	Fri	Sat	Sun
12.00 noon	Cooking + lunch	Cooking + lunch	Cooking + lunch	Cooking + lunch	Cooking + lunch	Cooking + lunch	Cooking + lunch
2.00 p.m.	Homework, children	Homework, children	Homework, children	Homework, children	Homework, children	Gardening	
3.00 p.m.	Laundry		Ironing	Shopping	Orthodontics, Timo	Cooking, baking	Football, Timo
4.00 p.m.	Dentist, Julia	Timo, extra tuition	Buying shoes, children	Timo, extra tuition	Julia, ballet	Timo, essay	
5.00 p.m.	Shopping	Julia, music school			Ironing		
6.00 p.m.	Evening meal	Evening meal	Evening meal	Evening meal	Evening meal		Visit from Granddad + Granny
7.00 p.m.	Timo, football		Gym	Stitching + mending	Jogging	Barbecue at Uli's	
8.00 p.m.	Reading, Timo	Parents' evening, Julia	Reading, Timo	Reading, Timo	Reading, Timo	Reading, Timo	Reading, Timo

"There's got to be a gap in here somewhere for an appointment with Frau Dehmer, the psychologist!" Having told her friend, Marianne, about Timo's poor performance in school, Marianne had suggested that she take him to Frau Dehmer and have him tested for dyslexia. Dyslexia – that's just what she needed!

Of course, it would be a relief to find out what was wrong with Timo, but when exactly was she supposed to do this? She worked mornings, and the afternoons were dedicated to helping the children – mainly Timo – with their homework, sometimes for hours on end. And she still had the housework to do! Timo also had to be brought to extra tuition in the afternoon twice a week. She read books with Timo, she showed Timo how to write an essay, and she explained him the rules of spelling – all a hundred times or more.

"Will he never get the hang of it?!" she thought in desperation. "We practise and practise, and read and read, every day it seems! He just doesn't get any better, and it's not doing him any good. He hardly has any time to himself – and you could say the same about me. It's just too much; both of us are continually exhausted! I just can't go on like this, and Timo cries all the time! Every now and then I think there's a big black cloud hanging over our family ..."

Maximum effort – minimum result

Families commonly suffer from this kind exhaustion and frustration. Dedicated, hard-working mothers doing *everything* for their children who, because of their dyslexia, cannot cope with ordinary school work. Consequently, these parents try even harder to attain improvements. They practise spelling rules, including in foreign languages, more intensely, with greater frequency than other parents do. They continually explain the rules of grammar. They put even more time aside to practise dictation and essays with their children. They buy books for their children and train reading with them. Despite this, the results achieved are in most cases almost always extremely disappointing. As a result, instruction intensifies even more and takes up more time, often private tutors are hired for extra lessons – but the results particularly in spelling continue to disappoint. The child, still shows little enthusiasm to read of their own volition. Mother and the entire family are completely out of their depth. Put simply, investing time, energy and very often a lot of money just does not pay off effectively enough.

Many parents ask themselves if there is any other way of tackling the problem. Is there a solution that enables you to achieve *better* results in overcoming dyslexia with *less* effort? The good news is: Yes, there is!

Neuronal connections

You will remember that the cause of dyslexia can be traced back to the immaturity of the relevant brain region. But what exactly do "immature" or "not fully mature" mean. It's quite simple: immature in this respect means that the nerve cells (or neurons) which are responsible for reading and writing in the brain are not yet adequately networked with each other.

> *The reading and writing center works together with other different brain regions which are responsible for hearing, sight and fine motor skills.*
>
> *These brain regions need to be connected to each other and, additionally, the connection between individual nerve cells in the reading and writing center must develop in a distinctive fashion.*
>
> *Only then can a person learn to read and write well. The connections in the brain mature through continuous and specific activation.*

You or your child can achieve this specific activation by continually absorbing and assimilating letters through the senses of sight, hearing and touch. The neural network is strengthened as a result through a variety of "channels". If working with only *one* sense, whether that be sight or only through hearing, the quality of the results achieved are diminished. The more varied the impulses, the more effectively can the letters be *imprinted.*

Does that sound complicated or even too strenuous? It isn't really. On the contrary, stimulating the maturation of the reading and writing center of the brain is really quite simple. All your child has to do is to type text from a book on the keyboard of a PC while simultaneously calling out the names of the letters phonetically. This method involves all three of the aforementioned senses.

Typing letters – what happens in the brain?

I would like to explain step by step here what happens in your child's brain when it is typing a text.

- Your child looks at the first letter of the first word, an example being the H in "Harry". *The eye sees* the letter H in the book. This impulse is then transmitted via the visual center to the center for reading and writing and stored there. However, this *occurs more than once!* Your child then looks at the keyboard and sees the letter H once again, meaning it has already visually absorbed the H twice. This occurs for the third time when it recognises this letter on the screen.

- Parallel to all this, the sense of *touch* is also stimulated. Your child presses the H key on the keyboard with the writing finger. This impulse is forwarded to the reading and writing center via the brain's motor center and also stored here.

- In addition, the sense of *hearing* is also activated, as your child pronounces the letter H *phonetically* while pressing the H key. It is important for your child to use the exact *phonetic values* of the letters, meaning "Huh" and not "Aitch", "n" and not "en", "b" and not "bee". The *sound* associated with the respective letter is transmitted to the hearing center during this, categorised there then passed on and "saved" in the reading and writing centre.

Consequently, this technique ensures that your child imprints each individual letter of "Harry" *five times* through the senses of sight, hearing and touch. Your child has therefore disassembled and reassembled the word again letter for letter in a brain-appropriate manner.

You might ask at this point why your child *types* the text instead of using handwriting. After all, motoric imprinting of the shape of letters is even better where your child writes letters by hand – isn't it?

No, it isn't! Via handwriting your child *joins* the letters up to each other often individual letters are not clearly recognisable as a result. In addition, your child does not pick up, *imprint* the letters as a result, but rather *places* them (in a manner of speaking) on the paper. No *absorption* occurs here, only *(weak) repetition*. Apart from this, some children suffering from dyslexia write in *mirror fashion* or another inaccurate manner. They tend to memorise the *wrong* symbols in such cases, rendering this exercise completely counter-productive. However, by typing, your child sees the letters *correctly and on three occasions*: on the original page, on the keyboard and in the typed text. This take up of individual letter information is more effective than merely writing a text in the vague hope of general improvement.

If your child breaks down the word into individual letters with the aid of the keyboard, numerous things happen in the brain as a result. The letter impulses received in the reading and writing center result in "triggering" of the nerve impulses in the synaptic gap between the brain cells. This stimulation increasingly accelerates activation of the synapses until the connections between neurons have achieved the strength and efficiency required for good reading and writing.

Without these connections, your child can go on practising to the point of complete despair – but still fail to learn to read and spell fluently, easily and competently. It simply cannot find the link between the symbol, sound and movement and, as a result, is unable to memorise individual letters efficiently (which are a combination of these elements). You will only achieve a real breakthrough through the take-up of individual letters *using different senses simultaneously*. Systematic typing is the simplest method to assure this development. And the result? Your child learns to read and spell just like other children!

Twenty minutes of training through typing each day will achieve much more than countless hours spent by your child doing other exercises which have been *proven* to achieve no measurable results, simply because they are neither brain friendly nor child friendly. Your child needs to imprint the individual letters every day using the three senses of sight, hearing and touch if the reading and writing center is to mature. Mindless practising and cramming is absolutely useless if the prerequisites for imprinting the written word are missing.

Maturity, maturity and maturity – nothing more, nothing less!

Extra tuition and courses for dyslexia sometimes achieve good results, but only if children type regularly on the PC or imprint letters at regular intervals via the three senses. However, children on courses of this kind usually only work in part with letters, which is why the majority of dyslexia courses only achieve partial success – if at all - depending on how often children imprint individual letters.

Given these results, you need not feel badly about cancelling extra tuition or courses for treating dyslexia you may have organised for your child. Aside from the money you will save, you'll also gain more time in your weekly schedule, and your child will also have more time to play with friends. It will only be necessary for them to type for 20 minutes on a daily basis.

And a child that plays is more relaxed, under a lot less pressure and able to concentrate better during the 20-minute training period.

Patience is required.

It will take time before daily typing training starts to bear fruit. Some children need three months before dictation marks improve, while others may take six months or an entire year. Quite often however, the child's performance and marks in school suddenly improve dramatically when the required brain connections are established. Your child's difficulties with reading and spelling simply vanish as if they had never existed in the first place! Your son or daughter is then no longer a "dyslexic", but a completely normal child devoid of any learning difficulties. And all this is achieved through a mere 20 minutes typing training a day!

The following step-by-step guide will show you (and your child) how to proceed and achieve success.

Four steps to successful reading and spelling

Step 1:   Typing letters

You will need a PC or laptop or a mechanical typewriter for typing training. Using a typewriter is even better, because a greater effort needs to be exerted to depress the keys. The impulse received by the motor center in the brain is even stronger as a result. But don't worry if you haven't got a mechanical typewriter – it works just as well with a PC!

For 20 minutes every day (including Saturday and Sunday), your child should type out a text you have selected from a book or other written source *always using the index finger of the writing hand*. *Never dictate the text!* Your child needs to be able to absorb the text themselves via the sense of sight, touch and hearing to ensure that the letters are imprinted individually.

As a rule, your child will soon appreciate that they are making fewer mistakes and reading better. Point out the improvements your child has achieved no matter how small. ALWAYS!

Step 2:   Saying letters out loud

During the first five minutes, your child should pronounce each letter phonetically on typing it, for example, say "b" and not "bee" and "f", but not "eff".

The phonetic pronunciation of letters can be heard at

- UK: https://www.youtube.com/watch?v=-ksblMiliA8

- USA : https://www.youtube.com/watch?v=Sx3QNVXyyKc

This helps you to ensure that the correct *phoneme* is linked to the *shape* of each letter in the reading and writing center of the brain.

A minimum effort here is rewarded by maximum improvement. Professor Wolfgang Schneider of the Department of Psychology at the University of Würzburg determined in a study of "phonological awareness" that children who receive phonetic support of this nature improve significantly in reading and spelling when compared to children who are *not* tutored in this manner.

Please note: practising phonetic pronunciation for longer than five minutes is usually too much for most children and slows down the working pace. It is also more important for your child to continue to type a further 15 minutes imprinting the individual letters visually and via the motor connection of the 'writing finger'. Please note that the index finger, which is used for writing with, forms, as do the other senses, a physical connection with the reading/writing center of the brain.

Step 3: Practising numbers and arithmetic operators

Following 20 minutes for typing training, give your child a few minutes to type the numbers from one to 10 and the arithmetic operators for plus, minus, multiply and divide (+ / − / x / ÷).

Dyslexics tend to read or write multi-digit numbers inversely (for example 41 instead of 14, or 526 instead of 625). Imprinting numbers on the memory through typing training can eliminate this problem.

Step 4: Correction

Now correct the typed text together with your child (if necessary). To do this, you can print out the finished text your child has typed and correct it with a green pen (green is chosen because red is the colour used by teachers, and your child will only associate too many negative experiences with it).

Alternatively, words which are written incorrectly can be marked directly on the PC with the highlighter option.

Wrongly typed words should then be typed correctly again immediately after the exercise, as it is otherwise inevitable that these errors will crop up again in the next dictation, vocabulary test or translation. So effective is this imprinting that, due to the child's dyslexia, the incorrectly typed words are memorised in exactly the same manner as the correct ones – unless your child superimposes the correct version on the incorrect imprinting!

Thus, it is very important for your child to type the incorrect word *completely* letter for letter once again and *not* simply use the correction function on the PC. Failure to do this will prevent the word being imprinted as a complete entity.

Your child therefore needs to take some time following the 20 minutes to write the incorrect words correctly once again. If they make mistakes yet again during this, they should type these words correctly one more time.

An added advantage: Homework can be done at the same time

Your child will soon notice that, with increased practise, they can type *more* text in a shorter time period, makes *fewer* mistakes and can read better. These improvements may well increase your child's enthusiasm for this important exercise. One of the characteristics of this specific developmental training is that good results are not always evident from one day to the next. It can take a few weeks or months before you and your child notice any significant difference.

Despite this, your child can be further motivated to practise by combining typing training and homework, thus ensuring that the former is not merely regarded as a further burden simply added to the latter. Homework in English, foreign languages and other subjects can be typed (or at least where the homework contains a text suitable for copying). In addition to saving time, your child's homework also improves in all other subjects.

This allows you to kill two birds with one stone. While your child is typing, they are memorising the letters and their reading and writing center is maturing. If, for example, Spanish vocabulary is typed they will learn this quicker and more reliably, and achieve better marks!

I will illustrate different options on the following pages which you can exploit to combine homework with typing training.

Homework: Copying text

Pupils are sometimes given homework which involves copying texts on a particular topic in order to learn the contents. In geography, for example, your child may have to copy a text dealing with the Earth's desert regions. Simply have your child type this text with the index finger of the writing hand instead of copying it in handwriting. The child can then print out the text and stick it into a copybook (or file it in a folder). You can also adopt the same approach in other subjects.

You should reach an agreement with the teachers in advance on the inclusion of these typed texts in the copybook or folder. Unfortunately, not every teacher will welcome this, but it's worth a try! In the event of a teacher raising any objections, your child should first type the text from the original and then write the typed version into the copybook. Your child has then done his/her homework while simultaneously completing his or her daily typing exercise.

Homework: Writing an essay

If your child is given an essay to write for homework (for example based on a picture story), you have probably noticed that they simply begin without taking a moment to think about what – and how – they want to write. Some pictures are described in far too much detail in a multitude of sentences, while others are covered in only a few words. It is quite possible that your child's thought processes simply do not match the pictures. Add to this the numerous spelling mistakes, and the results are often a confusing jumble which is rewarded with a poor mark.

There is a definite procedure you should take in such cases: Firstly, discuss what is happening in the story with your child. Keep the structure of the essay *simple*: introduction – main body – conclusion. Three concise sentences are usually adequate to describe each image in a picture story.

Then allow your child to draft the sentences, while at the same time typing them yourself on the PC. This will provide your child with a correctly written template. However, it is important not to impress your own ideas on your child or to "improve" their style too much when writing. The essay should still be the child's own work. *You* are only there to help with the methodical procedure of writing it down in an orderly manner, but not to create the essay itself. The teacher is bound to notice a style that just does not correspond to the age of your child.

After composing the essay together, your child can then type it from your original. Individual letters are continuously memorised and imprinted during this, at the same time this method allows you to teach your child how to develop an essay step by step. Your child will then learn to express their thoughts succinctly when telling a story, describing a picture or in discussions. You can use typing training to overcome their uncertainty and concerns when it comes to spelling and, in time, your child will no longer need your help and be able to master this task independently.

This method is just as effective for essays at any age. Whether your child is in the second or twelfth class, they will develop structure in their essays using this technique.

You can also use other exercises to improve your child's powers of expression and combine these with typing - more about these later.

Use of varied language

Children suffering from dyslexia often have difficulties when trying to write a colourful and exciting essay, frequently starting sentences with "Then ...". This phenomenon mainly originates from reading deficits. The child's vocabulary and range of variance in terms of syntax are not as great as with children who read regularly. Put briefly, dyslexic children have difficulties when it comes to expressing their thoughts in appropriate words and terms. A fear of making spelling mistakes prevents them from trying to write difficult words. Repeated failure dampens and impairs your child's self-confidence and, consequently, his or her performance.

I advise you to develop a range of options with your child which will help them begin sentences in a more varied style and ensure that the essay remains interesting. *Praise* your child and encourage them to find other terms and words. Allow your child to *relate* the essay to you. Develop suggestions for improvement together with your child and ensure that you *praise* their contributions. Create a new typing template for this new phrasing and expression and ensure that it is typed out – repeatedly. You can also print out this guide and hang it as a "poster" in your child's room.

Two objectives are involved here. Relating the story, enriching your child's vocabulary and stimulating their imagination will encourage them to write and, additionally, the new terminology is correctly anchored in your child's long-term memory through typing training.

For example, you could draft a list of alternatives to the word "then", with "now", "suddenly", "after this", "firstly", "all of a sudden" all being possible candidates. In addition to sentence beginnings, dyslexia sufferers frequently use the same expressions time and again for verbs and adjectives. In particular, the verb "to say" frequently appears on more than one occasion in every sentence. Essays really only come to life if colourful and expressive verbs are used. Alternatives to the verb "to say" could include "to think", "to whisper", "to call", "to talk", "to converse" or "to explain". You can also develop different verbs together with your child, while subsequently allowing them to type these out from your original typed template. Print out this list as a poster and hang it up in a position in which your child can see it whenever they want.

If we take an adjective such as "nice", you and your child can find a broad variety of alternatives such as "splendid", "outstanding", "fascinating", "enchanting", "attractive", "pretty" or "colourful". You should also print out this list as a poster.

Oh, and one more inside tip for you: Just *mark* a word in Microsoft Word, click it with the right-hand mouse button and select the "Synonyms" option with your cursor. A list of synonymous words then appears for selection − but remember: type them letter for letter!

*

Dyslexia can also frequently impair performance when it comes to *foreign languages* where, in addition to spelling mistakes, errors are made in grammar and translations due to reading difficulties. Word endings of significance in grammar are often read incorrectly or not at all, while words written or pronounced in a *similar* fashion are then spelt incorrectly

You can also use typing training for foreign languages to strengthen assimilation of vocabulary and learning of irregular verb tenses, grammar lessons and texts from a book which have to be read. The typing exercise is an excellent method when it comes to learning how to conjugate verbs.

Homework: Learning vocabulary

Your child is compiling a table with the latest vocabulary from the school book.

English	German
to see	sehen
The tree	Der Baum
...	...

The first column is sometimes in English, sometimes German. This alternation also encourages your child to think about the true meaning of words and better impresses these on their long-term memory − all of which improves your child's confidence for the next vocabulary test.

The words are copied through typing on a daily basis prior to a vocabulary test. Please ensure that the sequence is changed each time, as this encourages mental flexibility and not merely blunt learning by heart. If your child is then asked about an unusual word, there is a greater chance of them actually knowing the answer – and this will continue to be the case in later life!

We recommend this procedure for any tables which you see here, whether for vocabulary, the principle forms of irregular verbs or conjugating verbs.

Homework: **Principle forms of irregular verbs**

Your child is compiling a table again, this time involving principal forms of irregular verbs in German.

Infinitive German	Simple past	Past participle	Infinitive English
Gehen	ging	gegangen	to go
Essen	aß	gegessen	to eat

Your child now types all the irregular verbs from his German book into the table. Please *check* whether all the verb forms have been typed correctly.

Extra care must be taken to ensure that the irregular verbs are typed every day and as long as it takes for them to "sink in"! If vocabulary needs to be learnt at the same time, have your child type the irregular verbs and vocabulary alternately during the week.

Frequently used verbs are anchored more quickly in the memory than others, and verbs at the beginning and end of the list are imprinted more readily than those in the middle. For this reason, the sequence of verbs should be changed after a short period and, once again, have your child type these tables in an extra-large font size and print them out in bold typeface. Together with your child, position them as learning placards at different points around the house. Your child will then absorb these much better.

Homework: **Conjugating verbs**

The typing method is also an excellent tool to employ when it comes to conjugating verbs (e.g. in French).

être	to be
je suis	I am
tu es	you are
il / elle / on est	he / she / it is
nous sommes	we are
vous êtes	you are
ils / elles sont	they are

Homework: Learning the rules of grammar

Typing is an equally effective method for learning grammar rules. For example, take the case where your child types the rules for present perfect out of their German grammar book.

> *German speakers rely more on the present perfect tense when they're talking about the past. For example, in English we say: "I said", German: "ich habe gesagt"; habe = have, gesagt = said.*

Your child now types the conjugation for the *present perfect* several times a week from a verb conjugation table (usually found at the back of the grammar book). You then subsequently print out this sheet as a poster which your child can hang on the wall in, for example, the bathroom. The signal words can then be imprinted in a purely incidental manner when, for example, your child is cleaning their teeth.

> If your child employs the typing exercise *regularly* as a method to learn vocabulary and grammar, their performance in translations will continue to improve in a systematic and timely manner.

Homework: Translating

Five steps to successful translations:

1. Have your child read out and translate the individual sentences for you.

2. If your child is having difficulties with this, *you* should read the text out loud first.

3. If they are having difficulties understanding the text, get a vocabulary book and work through the text together with each other.

4. Allow your child to construct the translation, whilst you simultaneously type it on the PC.

5. After composing the text *together,* your child can then *copy it by typing* from your original.

Individual letters are continuously memorised and imprinted during this process, while your child simultaneously develops the ability to create a translation – step by step.

Homework: Reading and summarising texts

The majority of parents try to improve the reading ability of their dyslexic child through *reading*, but this an arduous approach, and as a method to develop relaxed reading, impractical! Your child suffering from dyslexia reads and reads, but it never voluntarily picks up a book. And why? Because they are confronted with *complete words* when reading which they often try to pick apart letter by letter with greater or lesser difficulty in an effort to understand them. This is a natural consequence of an immature reading and writing center in the brain which, similar to an underdeveloped muscle, is *incapable* of meeting the daily demands made upon it.

Imagine your child has an underdeveloped thigh muscle and is still expected to run a 100 m race every day. It's obvious what would happen –they come in last every time! And then suppose everybody, including you, said to them: "Come on, if you'd *practise* more, you'd be much better and be among the winners!" Your child would run and run, but the pain in the weak muscle would intensify and little progress would be made. This approach only leads to demoralisation. And so it is when your child is plagued with dyslexia and tries to read (and write). The prerequisites just are not there! However, you can create the conditions required – and with very little effort.

Having said all that: it is possible for dyslexic children, through hard work, *to extract* information from written texts. One should differentiate between the dyslexic child and the analphabetic.

During the typing exercise, the breaking up of words into individual letters and their imprinting in the brain's reading and writing center ensure the automatic recognition of words. Sequences of letters are automatically drawn together to form recognisable words. This works because nature always follows a particular sequence, starting with the smallest components (an entire "suite" of letters in this case).

This is a completely unconscious and automatic process. For example, do you have to *consider* how to put a picture of your surroundings together? You also take the combination of sounds to form words and, in turn, words to create sentences and arguments for granted because these background functions occur automatically, giving the brain more time to think and control your activities in a targeted fashion.

Put the reading exercises away and let your child *type* instead to encourage this word recognition function (the drawing together of letters) to mature and occur automatically as Mother Nature intended.

If your child has reading difficulties, you can help if you yourself as a parent *read out* the text which the child needs to learn for school and then discuss the content together. This will give them the chance to understand the contents of the text better and, most importantly, much quicker.

Your child also needs to *think for themselves* – which is the whole purpose of these exercises. Their intellect is enriched as a result, and both you and your child are spared the torture of time wasted laboriously correcting the latter's reading efforts. Allow your child to summarise the text whilst you simultaneously write it on the PC.

After composing the text together, your child can then copy it by typing from your correctly typed and printed-out original. Yet again and again individual letters are continuously memorised and imprinted during this process, and your child simultaneously develops the ability to create a step-by-step summary or abstract.

Use this method whenever your child needs to read and summarise a large section of text for homework. This procedure has proved most effective for "reading subjects" such as English, biology and history.

How to motivate your child for typing training

You may surmise: the majority of children don't want to type? The fact is, children often perceive typing to be an additional time-consuming and time-wasting task which has to be done before, during or after their homework. Aside from this, it's monotonous. So, be prepared to encounter resistance right from the beginning or after a month at the latest. This may not always be the case, but the resistance will increase over time.

Therefore, explain to your child that they are not stupid, but simply have trouble memorising letters correctly. Your child will probably point out that they already know these. React in a positive, encouraging manner: "Yes, you already know your letters. And if you learn to imprint these even more deeply, you'll become even better at reading and spelling, and your confidence will grow."

In other words, show your child the advantages of typing:

- Their marks in English and foreign languages will improve significantly.

- Far from being considered one of the poorest pupils in the class, your child will be easily able to keep up with the others.

- Your child will be able to demonstrate that they are not stupid, finally gaining the success and recognition they deserve.

- Your child will enjoy school more because it has more free time and better grades.

- They will no longer need to experience the frustration of trying but not succeeding. This method guarantees victory.

- However, be frank with your child and explain that it will take a while before the first improvement is scored, otherwise they will quickly become discouraged.

- You can stop doing tedious spelling and reading exercises immediately, and cancel extra tuition. In this case your child will have more leisure time right from the outset, and even more when they finally conquer their dyslexia.

- Your child will be able to doing homework and typing exercises at the same time, saving time and also improving their homework as a consequence.

- Your child will be able to *choose the job they want* and *pursue the career they desire*, being no longer hindered by poor results in school.

All of these arguments will probably be enough to convince your child at the moment, but they may no longer suffice when your child's *perseverance* with regard to typing exercises is put to the test. It is perfectly human to have difficulties overcoming our impatience and doubts when we have to deny ourselves something *now* for a *future* gain.

For example, you know yourself how often you have *not* managed to go jogging or to exercise regularly. Your child will probably become impatient and dissatisfied after a while and either forget to type or deliberately seek to avoid to. You can go some way towards preventing this by reaching an agreement with your child right from the outset.

The typing agreement

Far from being confined solely to you and your child, the typing training project involves the entire family. This is best achieved by having both parents and any siblings present for the first discussion about the implementation of the typing method. This meeting should take place in a pleasant atmosphere, and a few "sweeteners" in the form of your child's favourite cake or drink can be a very good idea.

There's no place for reprimanding, criticism or bickering here! It's all about a new start for the future, and your child is the center of attention.

Use this meeting to explain the advantages that regular typing training embodies for your child. You could then ask: "I'm sure you'd like to give it a try?" If your child says yes, both of you have practically won the battle. The important thing now is to seal this agreement, and this is best achieved by making typing a *ritual* anchored firmly in the daily routine.

You should therefore agree upon a time with your child at which to they will type every day. Your child should be the one to suggest this when and where.

Check and discuss the feasibility of their proposals. If, for example, your child expresses a wish to type late in the evening before going to bed, you could turn this down by saying: "Sure, typing before you go to bed would be an option. However, on the other hand, you won't want to type when you're tired. And you'll make more mistakes as a result and have to rewrite words more often. That's a lot of additional work for you! What about typing right after lunch? Then you'll have it over and done with. What do you think? Agreed?"

Experience has shown that a time selected early in the evening before the family has settled down is often best (. prior to the evening meal or before your child starts watching TV). This is because your child then adopts a particular rhythm and can expect to enjoy a "reward" for its efforts directly afterwards. Your child gets used to typing training before the evening meal or TV – and you also become accustomed to it. This ritual then becomes a fixed part of your family life.

You should then end this first meeting by summarising the results: "Okay, Lucas will type from the book "Harry Potter and the Philosopher's Stone"" for 20 minutes at 5 o'clock every evening, and directly after breakfast at the *weekend*. Mummy or Daddy will then check his typed work directly afterwards. We'll meet again this day next week to see how it has worked out. Same time, same place. Oh, and we'll write this agreement out and put it in a special folder. If there are any disagreements, we can simply look in it to see what we decided together. OK?"

If you have handled the meeting deftly and even-handedly and summarised the agreement well, there should be no objections.

Monitoring success is best

Monitoring of success is *absolutely decisive* for both you and your child, as you can record what went well and what could be improved on in future. Always approach these 'monitoring talks' in a positive manner. If your child only typed on four out of seven days last week, you could react as follows:

"Lucas, you've probably noticed that your reading is a little better recently. And if you keep this up, you'll soon have no problem with reading at all. Well done! Now then: we have a problem. You typed on four days last week, and that's all well and good. Unfortunately, you didn't do any typing on the other three days, *and* you were grumbling about it. That's a pity, because it breaks our agreement." (Please note: *always begin an evaluation positively the smallest improvement must be mentioned*)

You may well get a cheeky reply from your child, but keep calm and carry on, continue to press your argument. "You do know that training will only help if you type *every day*? What a shame a fine lad such as yourself. I'm a disappointed with you! Looking forwards I bet you have a suggestion as to how it will work out better this week. Don't you?"

Be resolute until the matter has been taken care of. Indulgence is the wrong stance here, because quite simply the psychological well-being and future of your child is at stake. Note this agreement in writing for your meeting next week. Your child will also learn the meaning and value of working systematically, consequence and endurance – as side effects.

To-do checklist

- *Always search for improvements, no matter how small and tell your child where and how much they have improved*

- Typing training has top priority. Nothing else is as imperative. Music, hobbies, sport and playing are important and all have their place in the life of your child. *Nevertheless, reading and writing come first.*

- Reach an agreement with your child that they will type for 20 minutes every day, including in foreign languages. Stick to this agreement and monitor it rigorously. Your child will thank you later for this.

- Ensure that both parents are involved in this plan and other family members are informed about it.

- Clearly illustrate the advantages your child will have when they type regularly.

- Use typing training for spelling tests, essays, texts to be learned, vocabulary and grammar (in foreign languages). This is much more effective, and you'll be delighted by the results!

- Always ensure that typing of text is done correctly – letter by letter using one finger, the index finger which guides the pen.

- Ensure that incorrectly written words are corrected by typing them letter by letter in the right sequence.

Typing is an *extremely effective training modus* and, essentially, you don't need anything else to overcome your child's dyslexia. But I do admit that your child may well find it pretty boring over time, having to repeatedly do the same thing. That is why I developed other methods to lend more variety to this biological maturation process. Your child can achieve the same fantastic success with this method and also have a lot of fun, you too!

This other method consists of *playing!* But not just any old games: these alphabet games help your child to imprint individual letters through the senses of sight, sound and hearing. In the following chapter, we will examine the colourful world of these games in greater detail.

5.   Alphabet soup

Games for better results

"Granddad, stop tickling me!" Jens giggled and twisted on the sofa.

"Granddad, can you tickle *me* too?" asked his seven-year-old sister Iris.

"Hey! You two! Can't either of you sit still?! I'm not tickling you, Jens, I'm just tracing on your back. I'm drawing letters of the alphabet ..."

"Okay Granddad, don't say what they are! Don't tell! That's not fair!" Iris interrupted again. "Jens should guess without any help, and then you can tickle *me*! Weeeeee!"

Iris jumped up and raced around the living room, followed closely by Jens. Wrestling Iris playfully to the floor, he traced a letter on her back and cried: "Here you are! t for tickling, t like tickling ...!"

These children may seem to be only playing about and having a lot of fun, but they are also *memorising letters* using the three senses of sight, hearing and touch. If Jens and Iris continue to play in this way, they will be rewarded in about *one* year when they have overcome their dyslexia.

I never grow tired of emphasising the fact that dyslexia can only be conquered by imprinting letters using different senses. I am *not* saying that practising letters through *typing training* is the only way to vastly improve the love of reading and to enable highly competent spelling. There are more creative ways to imprint letters, an example being through *games*.

There is a whole host of very good alphabet board games (such as *Junior Scrabble, Scrabble,* or *Boggle*) available to purchase online or in shops. However, we have also developed our *own* alphabet games at the *Kennedy Tutorial School* which overcome dyslexia, ensuring that letters are memorised through the senses in an ideal and playful manner. The difference to typing training is that these can be played in a group, which the children enjoy very much. They are fun, which in turn helps motivate your child when they play them with you and the rest of the family. These games can be played with very simple materials described below.

You can also play some of these games *without* any materials whatsoever. A little creativity can be used to expand alphabet games, and you will have no trouble discovering new variations yourself. Any variation which ensures the *imprinting* of individual letters through the senses of sight, touch and hearing are to be greatly welcomed.

Simple alphabet games (or, in the case of Scrabble, not so simple but effective) are an excellent form of motivation. If you try to do homework with your child, they will frequently feel they are "losing" the struggle, particularly with regard to reading fluently and spelling capably.

But when playing games, your child can *win*, the tables are then turned! Imagine you are playing an alphabet game with your child and they beat you three times in a row! Well, you can really show off your acting talents in this case, playing the helpless and despondent loser. Seeing this, your child will probably say: "Don't worry Mother, you'll get the hang of it. I'll show you how it works the next time!" This will work wonders for your child's self-confidence! And, even if your child does not win, they feel they have the same chance of winning the next time.

Whether you play a classic table game or a merry board game on the carpet is irrelevant, as the fact that your child has reading and spelling difficulties will not be noticed. Your child will be able to compete at the same level as their playmates. They will experience success and also accept failure, just as one would normally expect during light-hearted competitions. The net result is that your child enjoys both greater confidence and recognition.

Just take full advantage of the principle of equality and the fun of playing with the family! Your dyslexia child can play with and against Mummy and Daddy, Granddad and Grandmother and even friends. It's really enjoyable, and watch out! your child's requests for games of the alphabet are sure to increase. ☺

Should we play *as well as* or *instead of* typing?

Combine these alphabet games with the typing exercise every day, and your child's efforts to overcome dyslexia will result in greater enthusiasm. Just try to ensure that your child doesn't get bored; typing can be *supplemented/and or substituted* with games of this kind. For example, they could alternatively type on *one* evening and play on the *next*. Or your child can skip typing completely.

If truth be told, you will achieve the same positive results in reading and spelling if your child continually imprints *individual letters* by *playing* and using its senses of *sight, hearing and touch*. Twenty minutes of play each day is just as effective as 20 minutes typing. Your child may even refuse to stop playing these games – which is all the better!

The best thing about it is that you can play anywhere and at any time with your child, because these games and simple materials used can be carried anywhere and everywhere with ease.

Alphabet games – flexible fun

Take advantage of every opportunity to play alphabet games with your child, as often as possible and not only at home, but anywhere the chance arises.

Imagine you are in the paediatrician's waiting room and, well, waiting as usual! You won't have any time to get bored, though, because you have a game with you and are playing with your child. Or you can simply play these games for which you don't need any materials.

Or you are travelling by car or train ... and playing alphabet games. Or you are visiting relatives or friends ... Or your child is playing with friends. Your child's playmates will hardly notice that your child is dyslexic and, if any of these friends also have difficulties with reading and writing, they will also benefit from the experience! You can play on the carpet or in the garden, or even at parties! For example, the game *Alphabet Charades* is ideal for this. When you are on holidays, you can play on the beach in the sand or with seashells. If you are travelling in the city with your child, you can simply ask them to guess which objects you are thinking of based on their initial letters — and this game is also perfect for foreign languages!

Our 30 years of experience indicates that the majority of dyslexia sufferers can identify individual letters relatively well, so there are no real barriers to enjoying the games. Should you notice that your child has not yet reached the same level as others (regardless of age), then you (or a person you trust) should play with them until the individual letters of the alphabet can be reliably identified and they are ready to join in with other children. This is usually achieved very quickly.

Day in, day out, your child is memorising and assimilating letters through the three senses, over and over again. This continues until your child's dyslexia is a thing of the past! Whether this is achieved using a keyboard and/or through games is of secondary importance. The main thing is that letters are effectively imprinted!

However, *one* distinction needs to be made here. *Typing is the better choice where words, training dictations or foreign languages need to be learned by rote;* simultaneously two things are secured: the indentation of letters and the memorising of content that has to be learnt. Typing training is more economical in this case as it saves time and better results are achieved more quickly.

Invent your own games

You can also invent your own games with which, in addition to memorising letters, your child can go through its school material. For example, your child can go through the capitals of Europe in geography, practising their initial letters. During this, your child should write, say, an invisible P in the air (with the writing finger) while pronouncing "P" (phonetically p not pee). It should then name the capital city that begins with this letter: "Paris". Finally, your child should invent a funny sentence containing the word "Paris". It then continues the game in the same fashion with other capitals.

When it comes to history, your child could write an invisible letter such as N in the air, pronouncing the letter in a phonetically correct manner (N and not en). It should then name a historical person or event that begins with this letter, for example, Napoleon. You could then ask questions about Napoleon, with each question being developed from the last and the most important letter in each being written in the air. When did Napoleon live? A possible answer is at the time of the French Revolution, so the task is to write an r in the air! – How did Napoleon come to power? Write a p in the air! – And so the game continues.

You can invent games for every relevant subject in the same manner, and your child can:

- imprint and automate letters
- practise *verbal* skills
- simultaneously expand its knowledge

Remember:

- always ensure that the letters are pronounced *phonetically*
- and drawn in the air with the index finger of the writing hand – the more often the better.

7 Creative ABC games

I have included descriptions of seven games below which your child is bound to enjoy and which are very simple. Please ensure that the players always pronounce the individual letters phonetically simultaneously whilst playing (so, b and not bee, f and not eff) as described in the last chapter. This will ensure that your child imprints the letters optimally and overcomes their dyslexia – while at the same time having a good time doing it!

Game 1.   Marking Letters

Keep your eyes peeled in this game, because things are not necessarily all they appear to be! It's a game for two players. Your child hunts for letters which can be easily confused, and *you* help them to check whether everything has been found and correctly identified.

You can also use the game as a partner exercise or group competition in which the player who identifies the most letter pairs in the text wins!

Learning objective:

Accurate differentiation of letters which appear similar, sound similar or are written inversely.

Material:

- Two different coloured pens
- A copy of a page of text (from a reader, geography book, biology book or English book). Please enlarge the text if it is too small on the copy!

Object of the game:

Your child should be able to reliably identify all the letters in the text which could be easily confused with each other.

Procedure:

Choose a reading text and copy it, enlarging it if necessary.

a and o, i and j, f and t, f and r, h and b and q, k, b and p, m and n, n and u, h and n, p and b, d and b, p and q, u and n, and, are all letters which can be confused with each other.

Now select *one* pair of easily confused letters, for example d and b. Then use to two coloured pens to write the d in red and the b in blue *above* the text.

Now it's your child's turn. Your child should take the red pen and **mark** every d that it finds in the text with this colour. Taking the blue pen, it then marks every b in the text. Your child should be allowed as many attempts as it wishes if this helps it to find any letters which have not been previously noticed.

Game ending:

When your child is finished, go through the text again and mark any letters your child may have missed. Use another colour to the one your child has chosen. Then write the number of *correctly identified letters* and the number of errors under the text. Both you and your child should count out loud while you are doing this, adding

- the number of letters searched for which your child did *not* mark,
- the number of letters it marked that were not the letters to look for and
- the number of letters it marked with the wrong colour.

Please note: Begin with short texts, as your child will otherwise lose interest very quickly. You can also use the same text two or three times in the beginning and search for different letter pairs in it. The number of letters your child misses will decrease over time, and you can then use longer texts.

Keep the copies already checked in a folder. You can then show your child how they are missing increasingly fewer letters over time, something they will find immensely gratifying.

And please improvise! You can play this game on the train, in waiting rooms, using foreign languages and reading texts in other school subjects.

2.   Letter Guessing

A classic game where the entire family can join in! The game can be played by two people or in pairs. To begin with, it is best for the father and mother to play with the child, with any siblings joining in later.

Learning objectives:

- Imprinting letters using the three senses of sight, hearing and touch
- Promotion of letter memorising

Material:

None required.

Object of the game:

Identifying letters by touch.

Procedure:

Write an upper-case letter on your child's back (using block script). Your child now has to guess what the letter is and name it – using the phonetic pronunciation, of course. After this, it's your child's turn to write a letter on *your* back which you have to guess and name.

This game can also be easily expanded. For example, when your child has become adept at it, simply write the lower-case letters in *block script*, upper case letters in *cursive script* and, for particularly proficient children, add the lower-case letters in cursive script.

Game ending:

The game continues for as long as the players wish.

As a family game:

All family members stand in a row, one behind the other. The more people taking part, the greater the fun factor!

The person at the back (which is a role best taken by you!) should begin and write an upper-case letter in block script on the back of the person immediately in front. They have to guess the letter through this sensing (feeling) and then write it on the back of the person in front of *him or her*. The last person in the row writes the letter on a sheet of paper and shows it to the person who began the game. If the paper shows the correct letter, the order of players is changed so that everybody has a chance to start play by writing a letter.

Another variant:

Instead of writing the letter which is guessed on a sheet of paper (or *only* doing this), the first person in the row should think of an animal that begins with this letter. They should then mime this animal.

For example, let's say the letter which is guessed is A - an ant is then mimed and the other players have to guess what kind of animal is being illustrated.

To expand this game, it is also possible to use vocabulary (any word) in a foreign language (instead of the names of animals)!

*

Holiday games are always enjoyable on a long car journey, at the beach or in a holiday apartment. But really you can play the following games anywhere and, in addition to being a lot of fun, they also bring the family closer together.

3.   Letters in the Sand

This is a game for the beach where you can let your child draw letters in the sand. Nouns, verbs and adjectives need to be found for each letter.

Learning objectives:

Memorising and assimilation of letters using the three senses of sight, hearing and touch

Linking of letters to words and their meaning

Material

A beach or sand pit

Variant 1:   Let's look for nouns

Your child writes a letter a in printed script in the sand and thinks of a noun to go with it (such as apple). They then follow this with a b and think of another noun (like bubble). And so on.

Ensure that your child always pronounces the letters out loud – but phonetically.

Variant 2:   Let's look for verbs

Your child writes a letter a in the sand and thinks of a verb that begins with it (such as to ask).

Variant 3:   Let's look for adjectives

Your child writes a letter f in print in the sand and thinks of a suitable adjective that begins with it (such as funny)

Variant 4:   Let's go searching for things

You could, for example, say to your child: "Find me something beginning with the letter B!" Your child first writes the letter B or b in the sand and starts to look for an object. It might see a beach ball, to give an example. Oh, and remember: Your child only needs to point at the object, not bring it to you!

Variant 5: Bring me something beginning with the letter F or f!

Your child writes a letter f in the sand and then goes looking for an object. They could, for example, bring back a feather. You can even make a competition out of this game, with whoever finds the *most* words and objects deciding who should be buried next in the sand! The children will have fun because they are on the move all the time.

These games can also be played in the garden, a park or even in the living room.

4.   Alphabet Charades

This game is ideal on holidays or at the weekend, because the more players involved, all the more fun!

Learning objectives:

- Systematic memorising of individual letters using the senses of sight and hearing
- Promotion of word formation through linking of individual letters
- Broadening of vocabulary
- Boosting concentration

Material:

- Drawing pad and thick felt markers
- 10 game tokens (pebbles, Lego bricks or similar)

Object of the game:

The aim of this game is to guess what the other players are miming and then give the correct initial letter to the task.

Procedure:

You and your child should first write some lower-case letters on the drawing pad. You can mix cursive and block script styles, or play an initial round with block letters, followed by a round with cursive letters. As you will.

The drawing pad page with the lower-case letters is laid in the middle of the table.

The first player who wants to mime a task looks at the letters and thinks of an appropriate task beginning with one of these initial letters.

Examples:

b for bowling

d for diving

s for selling

t for thinking

This player then starts miming the task (without using any words). These efforts often lead to funny mistakes, because some tasks can be illustrated in different ways. For example, the same movement could be interpreted as walking, running or jogging.

The other players can guess by quickly placing a hand on the letter they have chosen (on the page in the middle of the table), drawing the letter on the table with the index finger of the writing hand, pronouncing it phonetically and then naming the task.

The player miming should shout "No!" if a wrong letter is chosen.

The game continues until the right letter and appropriate task are named. Whoever guesses a task correctly and places a hand on the right letter at the same time receives a pebble and is declared winner of this round.

The letter is then written on the table by all the players using the index finger of the writing hand while being pronounced phonetically. The game continues with the next player and the next charade.

Game ending:

Whoever is first to gather 5 tokens is the winner.

Variations for foreign languages:

The game is played in exactly the same manner but using words from the foreign language in question. Examples are:

English	French
to make	Faire
to come	Venir
to look	Regarder

Please note: The letters can be pronounced phonetically in each game version, including with foreign languages, and written on the table using the index finger of the writing hand. English pronunciation is used here to keep things simple.

5.   Number Plate Game

A game for long car journeys.

Learning objective:

- Systematic memorising of individual letters using the senses of sight and hearing
- Boosting of creativity

Material:

None required.

Object of the game:

Whoever can form the most words from letters on the registration number plates of cars passing by is the winner.

Procedure:

Everybody in the family (except for the driver, of course) tries to form words from the letters on the registration number plates of cars passing by. But be careful: the letters on the number plates should first be pronounced loudly and phonetically and written in the air! Only after this should the players think of words.

Example: A number plate with "CA" is seen. Everybody says the letters C and A while writing them, after which each player tries to think up a word (perhaps "Castle").

Game ending:

Whoever has found the *most* words formed from the letters on number plates driving past after seven minutes is the winner.

6. "I spy with my little eye" – but a little different this time!

This game is ideal for car journeys, while taking a walk or even when simply looking out the window.

Learning objective:

- Systematic memorising of individual letters using the senses of sight, hearing and touch
- Broadening of vocabulary

Material:

None required.

Object of the game:

The children look for things (or appropriate words) while driving along that relate to the letters of the alphabet.

Procedure:

Proceeding in alphabetical order, the children first look for words or things that begin with A, then with B and so on. The letters should also be pronounced first phonetically and then written in the air. After this, the search for words associated with the respective letter begins. However, *purely random* words cannot be picked. The words chosen must be objects which can be seen outside:

such as a for ambulance, b for bridge, etc.

In the case of a speedy car or train journey, your child discovering an object simply says the word, and the other children have to find it in the surrounding landscape before they have passed it.

Your child does not say the word associated with the thing it has found during a walk or a *slow* drive. They *describe* the object instead, and the other children have to guess what it is and find it in the surroundings.

To expand this game, players can use words from one or two foreign languages, but the *English* pronunciation of the letters is used for the sake of simplicity: so v for *voiture*, b for *baguette*, and so on.

7.   Word Chains

This group game can be played anywhere without the need for additional materials.

Learning objective:

- Broadening of vocabulary
- Assimilation of letters using the three senses of hearing, touch and sight

Material:

None required.

Object of the game:

To find compound words or words that are made up of words e.g. cupboard: cup – board).

Procedure:

The first player names a word which is a combination of two other words, an example being "motorboat". Then they say m for "motor", simultaneously writing the letter in the air. Your child then says b for "boat" and, once again, writes the letter in the air.

The next player now has to find a compound word that begins with "boat", an example being "boathouse".

The letters b for "boat" and h for "house" are now pronounced and written in the air at the same time. "House" is now the first part of the new word, and so the game continues.

Anybody who fails three times to find a compound word has lost and is disqualified.

Game ending:

The game is played until only *one* player remains – and they are then the winner.

As you can see, these games are very easy, and children really enjoy them because they have the chance to be creative while playing. When combined with typing training, these games are *extremely effective*. You will be able to *measure* your child's progress clearly on the basis of fewer spelling mistakes and a marked improvement in his or her reading ability and behaviour.

A great number of parents have written to me in the last 30 years and described how, together as a family, they overcame the misery of dyslexia through these simple alphabet and typing exercises. These families learnt the importance of sticking together and being there for each other when difficulties arose.

Their children have emerged stronger, more self-confident and changed for the better from this "literally" formative experience. You too can achieve these results and, in addition to the improvement in school marks, your family life will also profit immensely. And it's so simple! Your children will understand and appreciate your desire to help them, even if they don't show it. Consequently, you should guide them with *single-minded resolution to success.* The secret to achieving this with skill, savoir-faire and a dash of panache is revealed in the following chapter.

6.   "Okay Mother, I can do it!"

How to motivate your child

The Spanish book spun through the air before thudding against the wall. "I've had enough of this!" Leo was screaming with frustration. "I don't want to type this stupid vocabulary! I had to type yesterday, and the day before, and I'm sick of it. I want to play soccer now with Ben instead!"

"But you know you have to do your typing training, and alphabet games. I don't know how many times I've had to say that to you!" his mother cried out in exasperation. Leo marched with a determined look towards the door. Although she tried to stop him, he wasn't taking any nonsense from her, he exited the room, slamming the door behind him.

"Leo, come back here at once!" she shouted angrily. The only reply was a muffled thump as the front door also slams shut. "Exercises over, front door shut, Leo gone", she murmured softly.

When soccer rules

A circumstance can arise where even the most engrossing alphabet games are not even half as exciting as usual. This usually begins with a knock on the door, and there stands a friend with a big smile, a ball under his arm or an invitation to go swimming or play computer games together. That said: children don't even need to do anything specific together.

Many boys and girls just want to talk, hang out and spend time together without being bothered by adults and without any chores to do. This is perfectly normal and understandable. Situations like these can usually be handled by choosing a suitable time for letter training where children do not "chillax" together with their friends.

Things become even more difficult for parents if, after practising for weeks on end, no visible success has been achieved. Children then lose interest in continuing with typing training and alphabet games. The child's reaction is marked by increasing reluctance and, depending on their disposition, defiance, truculence or aggression, and is often prone to clowning about or showing off. Those of a gentler temperament react to the lack of success with increasing uncertainty and tearfulness.

The majority of children improve visibly in reading and spelling within the first four weeks of training. However, it may also take as long as 12 weeks before initial progress is noticeable, depending on the extent of the dyslexia.

Around 10% per cent of children need *12 months or longer* until the reading and writing function develops at all and good results are eventually achieved. But even *after* the first signs of success have been noted, it still takes a while before the brain center for reading and spelling **matures** completely. All in all, your child should type and play alphabet games for at least *one* year.

Children are quite likely to lose their appetite for this method. The usual reaction of many parents in such a situation is to win through by ordering their children around, coercing them or offering rewards. "It doesn't matter why – you're going to type and that's that!" – "If you don't play the alphabet games, you can forget about going to your friend's birthday party!" – "Please, if you try I'll give you €2 ..."

However, this is not gratifying, as your child does not really want to stick at it. You will notice that your child will refuse to do anything voluntarily if you are either continually forcing or sweettalking them to practise and play the alphabet games. And even if they practise and play, their efforts are usually unenthusiastic and grudging. Not much fun!

Some parents give up completely if orders, "intimidation" or bribes do not work, thus impairing their relationship with their child. In addition to creating a bad atmosphere which then pervades family life, they also lose face in the eyes of their children.

As a result, these troubles are compounded in the long term. More daring children react to failure in school and the criticism of parents and teachers with defiance and rebellion, and this behaviour not infrequently also ends in open aggression towards these figures in authority.

Pupils who need a lot of recognition frequently act the clown both at school and in the family. In this case your child tries to draw notice to itself through constantly being at loggerheads with parents and teachers. Adolescents look elsewhere for the admiration they so urgently need, including in such alternative activities such as smoking and alcohol.

The gentler spirits among them become increasingly uncertain and anxious in the face of their failures, and there is a danger that they may slip into the role of the misfit or outcast. Other schoolchildren (and siblings) sense this uncertainty and often react with rejection, the result being that such pupils frequently become mobbing victims.

Frequently, the child's previous circle of friends turns against them, shutting them out completely. They suffer as a result, and utterances such as "I don't want to live anymore" may then be heard more than once. These children are at risk. In these cases, depression is a familiar and dangerous companion. You should not hesitate to consult a specialist doctor, *whom you have faith in,* just to be on the safe side.

But things do not need to deteriorate to such extremes! It is within your power to avoid these various scenarios. What exactly can you do if your child does not want to practise anymore?

You have to reach out to your child so that, for their part, they develop an interest in typing training and, equally, persevere when it comes to playing alphabet games. Put simply, you need to build bridges! There are three steps involved here:

1. finding out what motivates your child

2. awakening its interest in practising

3. using positive criticism through motivational dialogue if setbacks occur

Step 1:   Find out what motivates your child

When do people do things with vigour and zest? When they are *asked* to do them? When they are *goaded* into doing them? When they are *compelled* to do them? Or when they are *ignored*? No: They do them when they *want* to do them themselves! In other words, when they are motivated.

Begging your child or ordering it around will never really motivate them. The impetus to do something always comes from within: your child has to want to do it.

> **Definition: Motivation is demonstrated in voluntary, targeted *action*.**

Consequently, if you want your child to listen to you and do the exercises, giving orders or organising their daily schedule simply is not enough. Your child must want to do these exercises themselves.

You have to motivate your child to adopt your goals so that they are turned into *their own* goals and they are willing to pursue them voluntarily! You think this is a contradiction in terms dear reader? Not at all! In this chapter, you will master this balancing act when you discover what exactly orientates, moves and **drives** your child on a personal level.

In the following exercises, you can then look for correlations between your child's own motivation, the targeted goal and establish a link to both. I would like to show you in this chapter how to win over your child in a fair and frank manner.

> Every person possesses a variety of different innate motivations, and your child is no exception. These can be divided into two groups, namely *action-orientated* motives which spur us on to achieve *success, recognition and fulfilment*, and *defensive* motives which strive to achieve security and also social acceptance within a group.

Your task as a parent is to help your child fulfil their innate *action-orientated* and defensive motives through, in this case, typing exercises and alphabet games. Fulfilling motives means success for your child, and success is fun!

Observe your child to discern which motives are most perceptible. This is very easy to do through monitoring during normal day-to-day activities.

Let's take a look at the three main *pro-active* motivators:

1.   **Self-Affirmation.** Does your child stubbornly persist at a task they have selected themselves, despite increasing difficulties, and then proudly show you the *results* of their efforts? "Self-affirmers" of this kind expect to receive praise for the **results** of their work. This praise is important, but of secondary significance, as the most important thing is that, having achieved their goal, *they can then pat themselves on the back!* they need and often want no audience.

2.   **Social Representation.** Watch to see if your child is seeking the *glowing and enthusiastic admiration* from the group which it feels part of — and that at every opportunity. Your child expects to receive *recognition and wonderment* from this group for their "performance". This behaviour mirrors the second *pro-active* motivator — social representation. People motivated in this manner exploit every opportunity to shine before the group and only select tasks according to this criterion.

3.   **Self-Fulfilment.** In contrast, this third *pro-active* motivator - the self-fulfilment motivated person couldn't really care less what other people think of their actions! It is the actual action, *the doing of the thing* that fulfils their motives. The creative task itself is the source of fulfilment.

Goal-attainment, praise and recognition are of secondary importance. The "self-fulfiller" is usually completely disinterested in that which is happening around them. *Paramount is the undertaking of creative action in itself.*

The Two Defensive Motivators

Both of these defensive motives are distinguished by a poorly developed sense of personal initiative, and the avoidance of risk reigns supreme.

1.   The **Security** motive leads your child to avoid any endeavours which may harbour risks. These children

continually ask what they should do and whether they are doing it right, just to be on the safe side.

2. **Social Acceptance.** In common with social representation, this second defensive motive, is also group-oriented, but with one very significant difference. Your child, motivated by social acceptance, integrates themselves into the group of its choice embedded as a "follower" or "fellow traveller"

They are almost desperate to be accepted by others, also against their better judgement. Even where they personally hold a different opinion to the majority of the group, they agree with the others in order to dispel any suspicions that they might be "different".

So then: how does the situation come about where your child actively tackles or refrains from performing a particular action (in our case typing exercises and alphabet games)? This depends on the degree to which the action corresponds to your child's motives.

If your child believes their motivational needs will be fulfilled through a particular action, they will act accordingly. However, should they believe that the action will not contribute anything towards fulfilment or even to the contrary, they will not carry it out.

In other words, you as a parent should ensure that your child identifies typing training and alphabet games as actions which will fulfil their motivational requirements.

The motivation profile

If you wish to motivate your child, you need to know which types of motives are indicated by particular behavioural traits. This can be achieved with the aid of a motivation profile.

The psychologist Herbert Leger developed a list of motivational manifestations which shape our actions in everyday life to aid identification of what he called the three pro-active and two defensive motivators as described above.

Pro-active motivators:

1. Self-affirmation

"Self-affirmers" have a need to prove themselves. They set their own goals and measure themselves against whether they achieve these or not. What is decisive here is success in terms of the targets which they have achieved.

The "self-affirmer" also expects to receive recognition from you: "Mom, Dad, I made a crane out of a thousand Lego bricks! Mom, look how I finished this puzzle! Isn't that great?" The main thing is that your child achieves its goal – it made the crane all on its own! A girl that persists in organising her dolls' corner until it is absolutely perfect and meets her satisfaction in every respect is also motivated in this way. She has achieved her objective and can now pat herself on the back with a feeling of enormous self-satisfaction.

Other distinctive features are also indicative of the self-affirmation motive:

Your child ...

- develops ambition, orients itself according to success in the outcome and regards difficulties as a personal challenge.

- sticks to decisions and sees them through after identifying with them.

- prefers to think for themselves and act independently.

- develops a dogged persistence when pursuing goals they have set themselves. This is especially illustrated through stubborn and aggressive behaviour when there is a risk of failure

- or irritating friends, parents or teachers without any consideration of the consequences for themselves (particularly if they believe their decisions and behaviour represent an obstacle to achieving an optimally successful outcome)

- Your child continually reverts to their own ideas and suggestions and tries to make these work

- is aware of their own value and performance, expecting to be praised accordingly and in the keeping of promises made to them

- frequently assumes that everybody else thinks as they do and, consequently, fails to demonstrate empathy, sensitivity and tolerance

- repeatedly acts like a steamroller in terms of their behaviour, believing as they do so that their own dedication is obvious to others

- lives for success. Sustained failure or palpable denial of accomplishment may, against their better judgement, lead them to tolerate the failures of others, but only because these deflect from their own poor standing.

- tends to have an exaggerated opinion of themselves. In cases where they get into difficulties as a result of their own actions, they try to "box" their way through. This frequently leads to even greater damage which cannot be repaired.

2. Social Representation

This motive is governed by the norms and values of the social group which your child regards as an important benchmark. They continually strive to occupy a position in the upper reaches, or better, the pinnacle of this social group.

Admiration is both expected and demanded from the social group your child selects. In this case, your child wants to build the *best* crane or organise the *loveliest* dolls' corner in their entire circle of friends and be recognised and praised as such by them all.

Other distinctive features of the motive Social Representation:

Your child ...

- develops a dynamism and dedication in all tasks and activities that signal **status**. However, other routine tasks and activities tend to result in procrastination, their passing on to others or a negligent approach, particularly if these are of an everyday nature.

- tries to score "spectacular" successes in areas which they find interesting because they are a confirmation of status (sometimes at the expense of others).

- selects tasks and activities according to these criteria.

- tends to highlight results of this nature and refer to them at every opportunity.

- tries to demean others, particularly in cases of "status competition".

- regards conflicts with parents or teachers as a good opportunity to 'distinguish' themselves (being also not averse to employing unfair means in this respect).

- pounces on every opportunity to represent the group in the eyes of the outside world.

- tends to take command without permission to do so

- is hardly receptive to criticism and corrections.

- tries to stand out in every situation.

- Where there is no opportunity to present themselves in the context of practical requirements, they try to stand out through banalities and absurdities.

3. Self-fulfilment

Creative action in itself is decisive for people motivated in this way. The achievement of goals, adulation and success is of secondary importance. These individualists are frequently creative and tinker about, paint, decorate, build, write, think, rearrange and embellish all on their own.

They try out a wide range of different options and frequently fail to finish things because they are not result-oriented.

Other distinctive features are also indicative of the self-fulfilment motive:

Your child ...

- sets its own goals and ideas out in as creative a form as possible, identifies rigorously with these and pursues them doggedly despite resistance and failures, often over a longer period of time.

- concentrates on the action of doing when it comes to their objectives and ideas. Whether this action leads to tangible success is of secondary importance.

- feels challenged by that which is new or different. Things of this nature stimulate your child to become active, to experiment and to try things out.

- endeavours to give form to an image in their mind. They favour the creative over the traditional in this respect, and tend to tinker and fiddle about.

- frequently forgets functional requirements (reality) when realising tasks and embellishing ideas.

- as a result, they are usually fixated on ideas (are reluctant to turn away from actions which they perceive to be important in favour of other real-world tasks that require fulfilment).

- regards additional system-oriented requirements to be unnecessary and a burden (they believe they apply to everybody else, but not to themselves).

- sparkles with myriad suggestions and proposals.

- cannot be seriously deflected from their chosen path or their ideas.

- is very little affected by disintegration, a lack of acceptance or hostility, as long as they can pursue their ideas and beliefs.

The three basic motives described above are regarded as *pro-active* motivators or *action-orientated* motives. They are motives that create an active drive to create and achieve.

Defensive motivators

Social Acceptance

This motive aims to prevent becoming an outsider or a misfit in a group.

It is also governed by the norms and values of the social group your child feels attached to but, in contrast to social representation, this motive seeks *acceptance* in this social group (that is, to avoid falling in any way into the role of the outsider or misfit). A position of rank within the group is *unimportant*.

Thus, the social acceptance motive – which is frequently consciously acted out as acceptance *in the group* – can be considered more defensive in nature.

Your child *refrains* from activity to avoid being expelled from the group. The norm prevailing in the group dictates that, in a situation where all other members of the group are wearing green shoes, your child has to do the same. If the leader of the group suddenly thinks xyzzy music is "bullshit", your child may well also say so, even though they really like this kind of music.

Other distinctive features also indicative of the social acceptance motivator are that:

Your child ...

- continually agrees and repeats the arguments of others, strengthening them as a result

- rarely says no to anybody, particularly in situations in which they shouldn't say yes (because of clearly discernible negative consequences for themselves, due to an obvious overburdening or because of infeasibility which is recognisable from the outset)

- always adapts to general moods and opinions, even where these are contrary to their own clearly expressed opinions stated beforehand

- avoids conflict if at all possible:

- - agrees to things and tends to promise a lot or even everything. - - when it comes to avoiding conflict, they do a lot of things alone, - secretly try to go their own way.

- frequently suffers under the excessive burden and lack of a systematic approach to work when doing homework or placates others with empty promises and assurances

- conceals their own criticism behind the assertions of others or behind apparently objective facts (such as experience, conclusions drawn from earlier situations of a similar nature, proven recipes, generally applicable statements).

Defensive motive: Safety

If this is your child's primary motivation, they continually strive to avoid risk. For example, your child always holds your hand when crossing the street.

The child may gaze for long periods at other children from the window, asking their mother whether they should join the others in play before finally daring tentatively to approach them and asking to play with them.

As a consequence, this motive frequently leads to your child refraining from activities more than actually participating in them. Your child continually seeks reassurance.

Other distinctive features are also indicative of the motive, security:

Your child ...

- often seeks reassurance, in spite of the fact that they are familiar with the facts

- is fond of routine tasks and routine procedures

- demands rules

- tries to procrastinate when faced with more difficult, new or risky decisions

- likes to obtain additional approval for decisions

It is not difficult to see that your understanding of how your child is motivated is of enormous significance. More daring children need successes, recognition, time and space to allow their creativity to unfold.

However, should your child exhibit a need for security and acceptance, it is also up to you ensure that this need is addressed. If these defensive motives are fulfilled, you can then work together with your child in the search for ways to achieve little by little, the success and recognition that we all desire.

Consequently, it is useful to make a simple *motivational-profile* of your child if you wish to be able positively influence their behaviour. The complete motivation profile takes all five motivators into consideration, because every single person embodies all of these motives to varying degrees.

I am continuing to draw upon the findings of the psychologist Herbert Leger in this respect.

If you wish to compile a *motivation-profile* for your child, then observe him or her closely. This is easy. First compile a list of your child's activities so you can categorise their behaviour according to motives. Ask yourself the following questions while doing this:

- What does my child like to do?
- Do they play on their own? Sometimes? Always?
- What do they play?
- When do they become insolent or aggressive?
- Do they expect praise for doing things?
- Do they expect to be admired?
- Do they want to shine out in front of others?
- Is my child creative, inventive?
- Do they forget about the outside world during the above?

- Who do they play with?

- How do they get on with their friends?

- What makes my child happy?

- What annoys them?

- What do they prefer not to do?

- What opinions do they have?

- Whose opinion do they advocate?

- What makes my child uncertain?

- What makes my child anxious?

- Do they always ask permission to do something?

Following this, compare your observations with the following examples. Each of them mirrors a particular motive. I have mixed up the sequence so that it is not immediately apparent which motivator is being described.

The solutions are given after example no. 5. Think. Which of these scenes most closely reflects your child's situation?

Example 1

Steven finally attended his first private piano tuition lesson today. However, following lengthy negotiations, his mother had to go with him, as he would otherwise not have attended due to the extreme anxiety he felt.

She found it more than a little embarrassing, as he insisted that she be present during the lesson. At last they agreed that she would wait outside the door, but, despite this, he repeatedly called out to her to see if she was still waiting outside.

Example 2

Every afternoon without fail, twelve-year-old Jack plays soccer with his friends. He's a very good player, and his playmates are constantly urging him to become a professional when he's older. Jack likes to recount this at every possible opportunity. He's captain of the soccer team at school.

Recently his friends have started to show a preference for chasing each other around on their bicycles instead of playing soccer. Jack's not as good at this game, and he blames this on his "wobbly" front wheel. He thinks his friends are boring, and he tells them this as well. So instead he now plays soccer every day with the boys from the soccer club.

Example 3

Christine is invited to Sophie's birthday party. Frau Fischer has found a pretty frock for her that really suits Christine and which she likes to wear. But not today! And it almost comes to tears as her mother tries to convince her to do just that. "Chris, you know how pretty you look in it, and you love wearing it otherwise!"

"Yes, but not today! Sophie and her girlfriends all wear tight jeans, and I don't have any!"

"But you don't like that style. That's what you told me last week – before you got the invitation!" said Frau Fischer, distractedly.

"Yes, but I want to wear jeans to Sophie's party. She and her friends all think jeans are really cool, and I don't want to be the only one there in a stupid frock. You want me to have friends too, don't you Mummy?"

Example 4

Ruth, who is nine years old, likes to paint colourful pictures. She spends a lot of time happily painting alone in her room, carefully trying to capture the image of a girl on a rocking chair in every little detail.

Her mother calls her to set the table. "I've more important things to be doing at the moment", she answers cheekily. The consequence of this is an argument between Anja and her mother. After the meal, Anja apologises to her mother and then proudly shows her the completed picture. Her mother praises her for her efforts, and Ruth happily skips away.

Example 5

Day in, day out, Teresa cuts and glues, sticks and stitches and joins a variety of materials together. The patterns she has created for her Indian carpet are colourful, varied and very unusual.

Every time her parents look in on her, they find she has changed the carpet again! "Well, dear, when will the carpet be finished", asks her mother. "I don't really know, someday soon", replies Teresa with a somewhat disinterested air. "First I want to try again to capture the colour of the sky with other things."

Solutions: example 1 = security, example 2 = social representation, example 3 = social acceptance, example 4 = self-affirmation, example 5 = self-fulfilment.

However, it is sometimes difficult to understand why people do what they do purely on the basis of their actions. Their motives become clearer if their *reaction* in the event of *not* achieving their *objectives* is observed.

The following table illustrates how, according to the Leger model, a child (or adult) reacts according to its motivational make-up if obstacles arise and it fails to reach its goal. It is a fascinating additional aid which can be used to identify your child's motives with greater clarity.

Motive	1st stage	2nd stage	Conclusion
Self-affirmation	Rejection Aggressiveness	Defiance Stubbornness	Aggression against the criticising person (such as mother, teacher)

Social representation	Self-justification Compensation	Criticism of the group	Recognition is sought in another group
Self-realisation	Inertia	Continues with activity -secretive behaviour	Seeks in a different location or disinterest
Safety	Evasion Pushes the matter away from him/herself	Formalisation (safeguarding, out of harm's way)	Acquiescence or aggressiveness *directed against oneself*
Social Acceptance	Justification Excuses Apparent adaptation	Evasion Flight	Resignation Self-pity Aggression or frustration

You can now compile a motivation profile for your child on this basis. Estimate in relation to each individual motive the percentage to which the respective characteristics apply to your child.

The strength of each motive is estimated with a percentage between 0 and 100 - each motive is assessed *individually*.

Example: Estimation for Martin (12 years old)

Self-affirmation: 80 %

Social representation: 70 %

Self-fulfilment: 15 %

Social acceptance: 30 %

Security: 10 %

> Martin's parent should ensure in this case that he can experience success in achieving goals (self-affirmation 80 %) and can shine in front of his friends or, in other words, his social group (social representation 70 %).

Let us assume that you now know your child's main motivators. It is then important to *link* these to the implementation of typing training and alphabet games right from the outset.

I will demonstrate below how you can reason with your child with regard to their motivational profile and how best to structure your *goal-orientated dialogue.*

Step 2: How you can make practising attractive for your child

This can be achieved through the *motivational dialogue.* This communication form demands from your child a specific *additional* task that has to be completed. Your child reacts with "Why?" and the objective here is to answer this as convincingly as possible, so as to encourage your child to type and play alphabet games enthusiastically from now on.

The motivational *dialogue*: Here's how to do it wrong

"Listen, Christian! I've read this great book in which it says that you only need to memorise letters to improve your reading and writing! This can also be achieved through playing. We can do it together!" said Frau Kimmich as she looked expectantly at her 11-year-old son.

"What do you mean? Letters? I *know* the letters, I'm not a baby or stupid!"

"No, no, you've got it wrong again. The thing is that this function needs to develop better in your brain. Everything seems to indicate that it is still underdeveloped. So, come what may, you're going to use this method aren't we!"

"Thanks very much, Mama, but there's nothing wrong with my brain! And as for this new method, we'll just have to see about that, won't we!" With that, Christian ran out of the room, slamming the door behind him.

What went wrong with this conversation? – The answer: just about everything!

The structure of a dialogue with:

- introduction
- addressing of the problem
- mutual development of a solution
- summary and conclusion

was simply not evident.

The *manner of communication* was wholly unsuitable, with no real communication taking place between the two. The mother just fired ahead, telling Christian what she wanted him to do and practically ignoring his reaction. His reaction to this was defiance.

Verbal reasoning techniques were almost completely absent. Frau Kimmich only focused on her son when she wanted to explain to him that something was not quite right with his brain. No surprise that he felt under attack as a result!

The motivational dialogue: Here's the right way:

In contrast to a chat, a dialogue in this sense, is always goal-oriented. It is your objective to win over your child's enthusiasm for typing exercises and alphabet games, which is why the 'discussion' should be structured.

Positive introduction

You should always launch a motivational dialogue in a *positive* manner. Using an **example**, you can show your child what they are capable of achieving or how likeable or constructive they can be (beware: no flattery!). Your aim is to connect with and awaken this energy.

This is important, as only too frequently the *problem* is immediately addressed at the beginning of the conversation, and your child feels immediately under attack. With a positive introduction, *your child is then the positive focus of the dialogue.*

Addressing the problem

Avoid accusations. You should illustrate the problem as a *shared* situation and name it clearly. Be receptive to any objections your child makes, showing understanding for their opinion without reinforcing it.

Finding a solution together

This phase of the dialogue is frequently the longest, and it is particularly important for your reasoning be in line with your child's *motivational profile*. In other words, you should show your child that typing exercises and alphabet games will contribute to fulfilment of their motivational needs: **success, recognition and safety**.

You should refrain from trying to impose. Work instead with suggestions and examples. Show understanding for any objections your child may have, and reason with them, employing the "if, then" strategy ("if you do this, then you will achieve that").

Also allow your child to propose solutions, as this will give them an opportunity of ownership. You can then see whether their proposals will contribute to achieving the commonly defined goal.

If they do, it is imperative that these suggestions be employed as part of the agreement. If not, explain why using the "if, then" strategy and offer your own suggestion.

If the child's proposals for a solution do contribute to achieving the objective but are in themselves partially inadequate, supplement them with your own suggestions.

Summary

Summarise the results of the dialogue and secure these with "Okay?" or "Agreed?" to make sure that your child and any others involved are in accord with what has been agreed upon. This should be achieved if you have conducted the dialogue openly and your reasoning has been skilful. You can then record the result in writing.

Success monitoring

Safeguard the measures by agreeing to a system of success monitoring from the outset and designating a firm date for this (such as after *one* week in each case).

For example, I would like to describe a motivational dialogue with an "pro-actively motivated" child. Let us assume that the results of the motivational analysis are as follows:

- Self-affirmation: 80 %
- Social representation: 65 %
- Self-fulfilment: 15 %
- Social acceptance: 40 %
- Security: 30 %

You will notice that successes are important for this child, and they want to achieve them for themselves. Of secondary importance, but also significant is their need for recognition and admiration in the group. The motivational dialogue should now be conducted in line with these pro-active motivators.

Example: Christian Schnell

An indication of how this can be done is illustrated in the following conversation between Christian, a pro-active motivated 11-year-old boy, and his parents.

Positive introduction

Mother: "Christian, please sit down with us here for a moment. Do you remember that time when you wanted to build a hut in the garden using branches, leaves and even the floorboards from the workshop? You almost cried with rage when it kept falling apart. But you kept at it until the hut was finished. Your friends were thrilled, and so were your Papa and I."

Addressing the problem

Father: "Now listen, we've got a problem: we need you to show this determination again! You know, your reading and spelling in school could be a lot better, even though we've tried everything to help you."

Christian: "I know it really gets on my nerves as does Mr Smith; he can't explain the rules at all. And the others in the class just keep...."

Finding a solution together

Mother: "Slow down Chris. Look, I think I've found a good solution that's just right for a determined guy like you who doesn't just give up at the first hurdle. And the method you can use to improve your reading and spelling skills is really easy. All you need to do is type texts out and/or play alphabet games every day."

Christian: "Why alphabet games?"

Mother: "The problem is with the letters, because you haven't memorised them properly."

"Now just a minute! I'm not a baby, and apart from that, I *know* all the letters. Would you like me to write the alphabet out while you watch?"

Mother: "I *understand* what you're trying to say, Christian. Of course, you know your letters. But the fact is that they need to be imprinted even deeper and stronger in your long-term memory bank – just like programs on a computer hard drive.

And when this adjustment is secured, the program runs automatically to set and identify the right letters in the correct order, imagine writing a dictation and getting a 1 for it, and being able to read much better than the other children. You can do it! You can prove to yourself and everybody else just what you're capable of! And it only takes twenty minutes a day to achieve this."

Christian: "I don't know, I mean, I've still got to do my homework, and then another twenty minutes each day on top of that – I won't have much time left for myself."

Mother: "Well yes, I understand you point. Okay, we'll do it this way: From now on, we'll forget all our supplementary reading and spelling exercises.

Secondly, to save time I'll read everything out to you in other subjects, and we'll turn it into a question-and-answer quiz. Thirdly, I won't grumble anymore about essays after you have written them. I'll help you with the structure. This method is also really great for this! And you'll save time in the end."

Father: "I'm sure you've got some ideas about how we can use these typing exercises to your advantage for your homework. Come on, think of a few!"

Christian: "Yeah, well, I'm not sure. Could I type out French and English as well?"

Mother: "Yes, that's a great idea! If you do that, we're sure you'll get better results a lot quicker! And, *last but not least*, I'll ask your class teacher if you can also hand in your homework *typed*."

Christian: "Well I wish you a lot of luck with that one, Mama!"

Father: "Okay Chris, when will we start?"

Christian: "Well, definitely not today! Maybe tomorrow?"

Summary

Father Schnell: "That's great, I'll take your word for it! Tomorrow, and every day, you'll type at three in the afternoon and play alphabet games for 20 minutes, okay?"

Christian: "Yeah, okay, don't pile it on. But I've got something else to do now ..."

Monitoring Success

Mother: "Good. I'll make a note of what we have agreed upon, ok?

Christian: "Okay, Mama."

"Now, same time, same place next week we'll check and review to see just how well we're keeping to this agreement. Okay?"

Christian: "Okay, Mama."

Mother: "Super, I'm really proud of you and you know what? This is going to get results!"

Radiate confidence – your child is sure to pick it up! Record this agreement accurately in writing and read it out at the next meeting.

I purposely selected a pro-actively success motivated child in this example, because these children are the most difficult to convince. *Defensively* motivated children are more inclined to do that which their parents wish them to do. The dialogue with them is, in principle, conducted in the same manner, but you should select other arguments and take more time to *encourage* your child and give them a feeling of security and support.

The other objective here is to arouse the *pro-active* motives in your child and to bring them out of the defensive and into the offensive-mode. Your child should *not do it for you*, but for themselves

I have listed the most important arguments for each motive in the following table. You can employ these to convince a child. In addition, it also contains objections which your child may have, along with suitable answers with which you can address these objections in a positive manner while continuing to reason with the child.

Motive:	Parents' argument:	Child's objection:	Positive uptake/ Further argument:
Self-affirmation	You can achieve success with this method.	I can't do this.	Yes, you can, and we'll help you. If we do it together, you'll be unbeatable!

	Show your classmates just what you're capable of!	I don't care what those idiots think.	I can imagine that the others get on your nerves. But prove to yourself that you can do it!
	Ten fewer mistakes in dictation, that's a target worth achieving.	You always want me to do so much!	Because you're so important to me. If anybody can do it, then you can! Show what you're capable of.
Social Representation	You will be one of the best in the class.	The class stinks.	I can understand your disillusionment. If you keep at it, you'll get to where you should be – right at the top!
	School will be a lot more fun if you have better marks in English and Spanish	I don't care about that; I can have fun when I'm dancing.	I see. How about fun and amazement in the disco *and* at school? That would be the perfect mix, and you can achieve both!
	You want to go to secondary school? (or university, depending on the age of the child).	There's nothing that great about secondary school / university.	Maybe you're right. But if you type regularly, you can *choose* where **YOU** want to go.

Self-fulfilment	You can develop your creativity even further using this method.	That's not so important. I'm also not very bothered by the dyslexia.	I find you calmness really impressive! Combine it with typing, and you'll be able to express your ideas even better! I'll help you.
	You're a creative person. All these mistakes just diminish your performance, you can change this.	Typing every day and playing the same games will be boring – the same thing every day!	You can play really creative alphabet games, and think up a few of your own. If you can read and spell better, you will find it easier to develop your ideas – along with having more time for your thoughts and concepts.
Social acceptance	This method will help you achieve marks that are just as good as those of your friends.	Yeah, okay, *even more* work. Nobody wants me to have any fun in this life!	Oh, you poor thing! Come on, cheer up! If you practise regularly, you'll be successful in the end and have more free time for yourself and your friends. We'll do this together.
	You can go to secondary school / university, just like the others.	I'll never be able to do that, it's much too much for me.	I appreciate that you think it is a lot. If you tackle this step by step, you'll get there very nicely and you'll be delighted just like your friends. Now come on!!

| | Typing and alphabet games will get you better marks, and that's fun. | It's just more work! I've already got tons of homework that I have to do correctly. How am I supposed to do this too? | I understand your concerns, but don't worry, we'll do this together. And I'll speak with your class teacher. |
| Safety | This method will really ensure that you make less mistakes, and you'll have more fun at school. | Okay, I'll do it at some stage. | Precisely – how about right now. Come on, let's get down to work to make sure you're safe and sound!! |

Step 3: How to reprimand your child without demotivating it

To monitor the level of success, make a note how often your child practises in accordance with the agreement, and how often they do not. It is also *imperative* to note your child's improvements in reading and writing in this respect – *including small ones!* This will ensure that both you and your child have increasing evidence that the problem is more and more under control, and that you are not at the mercy of the problem!

Time and again we see that, although children practice typing and playing day in, day out, they unfortunately still get a 6! However, if we look closer, we see that your child no longer makes 30 mistakes in dictation, but only 20 – and nobody says anything!!

In other words, a 30% improvement is evident, but this is not officially appreciated by teachers and sometimes missed by the parents. It is therefore even more **imperative** for you yourself to recognise improvements.

When it comes to spelling, it is the number of mistakes which is indicative of your child's progress. In this case, there is only one thing to do: give praise, and lots of it!

The emphasis with regard to monitoring your child's success is always on that which your child has done. For example, if they have typed on four days and then not on three, you should evaluate this effort as positive: "You typed on four days, that's good!"

You should then indicate that the other three days were a wasted opportunity, there is still more to be achieved and the agreement must be kept in full. Tell your child that you are disappointed – not personally in the child, but in its behaviour.

Encourage your child to make proposals for improvements. These, in turn, should be noted for the next talk. So, keep record in a folder specifically named Monitoring (your child's name) Success

How to Criticise

First, here's how not to:

"Okay Christian, you, lazybones!" his father says to the boy in a provocative tone of voice. "Why are you constantly moaning about this typing exercise? Your mother has told you a thousand times that you have to do it. I'm getting a little bit tired of your tantrums every evening.

Do you realise just how hard and long *I* have to work every day, just so you can have an iPad, an iPhone and now a brand-new bicycle? Well? Do you really appreciate what that entails? Your mother also works every day, and all you ever do is run off like a little child.

From now on, you're going to type, and as far as I'm concerned, you'll play those weird alphabet games every day. Now get out of my sight! Go to your room and think about what you need to do to improve yourself!"

Christian meets his mother in front of the door to his room. She is almost in tears. "Chris, please don't behave like this, there's a dear, okay? We only want what's best for you. You don't want to fall behind and have to do part-time jobs after you've finished school for the rest of your life, do you? You know what? If you do what we want you to, you can choose a new TV for your bedroom, okay?" she says in a trembling voice.

Christian pulls back his shoulders. "Well okay, but then I want the PlayStation XXL+ to go with it!" he replies cheekily.

This rather exaggerated example illustrates the type of mistakes parents often make.

The *manner of communication*: The father talked incessantly, made accusations and gave orders. He didn't let Christian get a word in. He didn't even stop to check whether what he said had been received and understood by Christian.

The mother only let Christian speak after she had catapulted him into a power position with her bribery attempt – which, of course, he took immediate advantage of!

The *rhetorical techniques*: To be honest, there was a complete absence of dialogue structure. The father made a speech, an aimless monologue. The mother ceded what was left of her diminishing authority by begging instead of reasoning.

The *structure of a dialogue* with an introduction, addressing of the problem, the solution and a summary was non-evident. Aside from this, no success monitoring was agreed upon. Failure guaranteed!

How to criticise fairly and effectively

You should employ a *critical dialogue technique* if your child fails to honour agreements. In other words, use it if the mutual plan for regular typing and playing of alphabet games is at risk.

Seen as a motivational instrument (in spite of its title), the critical dialogue is also a mutual search for solutions. The structure remains the same as with the motivational dialogue, with:

- introduction
- illustration of the problem

- mutual search for a solution

- summary and success monitoring.

Example: Critical Dialogue with the pro-actively motivated Christian Wagner

Positive introduction

Mother: "Chris, good that you're here! Take a seat. Would you like a glass of something? That was a super cup game on Saturday! Your lot played really well, even though the other side is in the league above your team, and you almost won! You really led your team well. Well done, Chris, Papa and I are really proud of you!"

Christian: "Thanks, Mama, thank you Papa, and it was nice that both of you could come to the game, your support was great!"

Addressing the problem

Mother: "We were happy to be there, my boy! Eh, Christian, we've got a problem."

Christian: "What's wrong, Mama?"

"Chris, you didn't want to do your typing training yesterday afternoon, and when I asked you about it, you simply exploded and then cleared off to play soccer with your friends! To be quite frank, you haven't shown much of an inclination to type or play alphabet games recently. I find that very disappointing."

Christian: "Yes, well, I didn't mean it the way it seemed, Mama, but this typing training is really getting on my nerves!"

Mother: "I can imagine, Chris, but everything has its price. If you don't stick to it, your marks in German will remain poor, not to mention English and Spanish. And it's questionable whether you'll pass your final school examination with good marks. In fact, it's unsure whether you'll pass at all. What do you think the consequences of having bad results or failing the examination would be?

Christian: "That won't happen! I want to be an engineer, and I need good marks in this exam and I want to study in Konstanz!"

Finding a solution together

Father: "You see, and that's why we're sitting here together to help you. Engineers have to read a lot of books too. If you fail to achieve your own goals, you'll be terribly, terribly disappointed in yourself."

Christian: "Yeah, and I certainly don't want to be the worst among my friends, with miserable exam results!"

Father: "Well good, then you have to type and imprint the letters continually."

Christian: "But I've been doing that for months and it's no help!"

Mother: "Now take it easy, let's take a closer look at this together. You're now making a lot fewer spelling mistakes. You used to make more than 35 mistakes in each essay, but last week there were only 12! You're also making excellent progress in English and you obviously understand the grammar much better."

Christian: "Yes, when you look at it that way, you're right, Mama, but the mark for the English essay wasn't any better than before."

Mother: "I can understand your disappointment. But if you stick to it, your marks for essays will also improve over time. The fact that you hardly used to read is also relevant. I mean, you've noticed yourself that you now pick up a book much more often. That's really super! And it will soon pay off for you in the form of better essays!"

After dealing with the teenager's objections, the search to find a solution together can continue.

Mother: "Okay Chris. I'm sure you have a suggestion as to how we can rid ourselves of the problem with the typing exercise and alphabet games that are not being done!"

Christian: "Yeah! Okay, I'll do my typing, without complaining, or should we play a game. Could we not buy *Scrabble*? It's a bit more challenging!"

Father: "We can do that, if you like."

Summary

Mother: "Great, Christian! Let me just summarise what we have noted and agreed. Your spelling has really improved immensely, and you're reading more. You're going to continue to do the alphabet exercises every day – without complaining or grumbling."

Christian: "Okay, Mama. And I'm sorry about yesterday."

Mother: "Very well. If you keep this up, you'll be sure to be at university Konstanz studying engineering in 18 months. We're absolutely convinced that you can do it!"

Success monitoring

Father: "Okay. I suggest we meet again in a week at the same time to see how well things have worked out. Okay? Agreed? Good, Chris, then give it your best! If you stick to it until the end of the year, then maybe we can talk about that new laptop that you would like."

Conclusion

When conducting this dialogue, always strive to achieve a solution which comes from your child. If none is forthcoming, then make a suggestion which gives them the opportunity to fulfil his motives.

In the event of negative behaviour, depict this as a self-impediment for your child. Using positive comparative examples, illustrate the areas in which your child is good (sport, skills when working with their hands, talent when playing, painting and in puzzles, etc.).

Look also for examples in the area of social behaviour, such as an affectionate relationship with animals or siblings, occasions where, for example, your child showed they were friendly or helpful. Draw on at least two examples as a contrast to any point of criticism you make.

Summarise the agreed measures and determine when they should be checked. This success monitoring should *always* be realised in a *positive* manner. The motto should be: "What was good, and what could be better?"

The first improvements with typing training and alphabet games are usually apparent after four weeks. In most cases, your child begins to read better, and the number of spelling mistakes diminishes.

In this regard, it is *your* task to observe your child attentively at all times to determine any improvements of this kind, regardless of how minor these may be. If you show these to your child, they then have measurable proof that their efforts are paying off.

A child can rapidly lose interest if they notice that they are not improving. In other words, you must motivate your child further until the promised improvements become apparent.

Even after this, you should continue to look for evidence that shows that your child is still making progress, and then praise them for this. If your child starts to read better than before, then praise them emphatically and show them why. You and your child are on the right path!

Experience shows that a child needs at least *one* year until they have mastered their dyslexia. Be on the alert when your child starts with the first or second foreign language, as reading and spelling difficulties may resurface. In this case, have your child take up typing training (especially for vocabulary and grammar) and the alphabet games again, preferably immediately at the introduction of the new foreign language.

Doing this will help you win the cooperation of your child. But what about their teachers?

7. Partners or adversaries?

How to get teachers on board – without capsizing

"Damn it, Herr Schubert simply refuses to see the progress Lars has made!" Frau Wilhelm handed her husband her son's dictation exercise book sat down, leant back in her chair and waited for his reaction. Herr Schubert glanced over the last page.

"Yes, it doesn't look so good, does it? He got a 6 again!"

"Take a closer look. Lars only made 13 mistakes this time!" Herr Wilhelm carefully counted the errors, nodding whilst an impressed expression spread slowly over his friendly face.

"Wow! Only four months ago he was making well over 20 mistakes! and despite this, he still only got a 6. That's very hard. What did Herr Schubert say?"

"Nothing, I'm afraid." Frau Wilhelm poured out a glass of red wine, offering her husband one as well. He shook his head. "It's just not right. I mean, the boy is really making great progress typing and playing the letter games regularly!"

"You can say that again! And Lars is lying on his bed at the moment reading the book his granny gave him!"

"Super, at last we're getting somewhere!" said Herr Wilhelm with relief and gazed questioningly at his wife. "But will it be enough to get him into Gymnasium (higher secondary school)?"

"I think so," she replied, "but we've got to get his class teacher, Herr Schubert, on our side. If he's to give us the support we need it's important that he assesses Lars' condition more accurately. He's got to encourage the boy to continue on with this method.

Apart from that, Lars has a lot of homework. It would be a big help if he could also hand it in typed. If we could get the school to work with us, we'd reach our targets much quicker and easier."

*

Actively encourage the teacher to *cooperate*; so that they, as a specialist, can support and motivate your child to stick with their training exercises. The chances of success are considerably enhanced if your child feels they are being encouraged from all sides. Progress will then be made at full steam rather than a slower pace. Both sides can then use this progress as fuel to power the "overcoming dyslexia" project on to further and even greater success.

Again: our aim is for your child to overcome their reading and spelling disability completely.

Parents today have a better chance of winning the teacher's support to help their child than could ever have been hoped for a decade or two ago. The world of education is in a state of change. in the past children were all too readily labelled as dumb or, indeed, clever on the basis of their results in dictation and their reading abilities.

However, many teachers today have at least a rough concept of what dyslexia is; the challenge they face is that they often have no effective "tools" at hand, or they persist in applying methods that are ineffective.

You as a parent need to be alert to this if you want to ensure that your children learn to read and write competently. The school system may toss and turn in whatever direction it wishes – at this rate it will never succeed in mastering the problem of dyslexia.

The latest studies also confirm this. For example, Wolfgang Steinig, a professor of German Studies at the University of Siegen, compared school essays over three decades with each other (cf. *Der Spiegel*, issue no. 25 of 17.6.2013) and concluded that, in comparison to 40 years ago, pupils make more than *twice* the number of spelling mistakes in essays today.

The results uncovered in this study were, in his own words, "dramatic". What *is* positive is that children show greater imagination and creativeness in their writing than before, a fact noted in a *Spiegel online* documentary on German television examining how well schoolchildren can spell - which was broadcasted in June 2013 (*Rechtschreibung bei Schülern: 'Ich fant den Film gemein'*).

Of interest is the development in terms of the *average* number of mistakes made per 100 words by *all* the children tested:

1972	2002	2012
6.94 mistakes	12.26 mistakes	16.89 mistakes

According to Professor Steinig, the gap between social classes has also widened, with children from educationally deprived families making considerably more mistakes than 40 years ago. Whereas the average in 1972 was 7.23 - 20.47 mistakes are being counted for every 100 words today.

The simple explanation for this development is the fact that a greater emphasis is placed by schools today on creativity in essays, with less importance being attached to spelling. Comparable findings are unfortunately not available for unpractised spelling tests. This would enable a direct comparison of spelling skills. Regardless of this, the study indicates that, in general, the spelling skills of pupils are not what they should be. This was a report made some years ago and, unfortunately, things haven't changed for the better.

These days an abundance of new methods are tried out in schools and many teachers (but not all) working nowadays are more open and flexible when it comes to new ideas. In Germany in particular a positive attitude to the concerns of parents are in evidence. Instead of rejecting parents' worries out of hand (which was frequently the case before), many teachers today endeavour to take these concerns seriously and do what they can to help.

It should not be forgotten that teachers are often overworked, dedicating a lot of time and effort to the preparation of lessons and correcting class work. A parent-teacher meeting is not infrequently regarded as an additional burden.

If you wish to achieve your goal, it is important that you display self-confidence and are well prepared when attending such a meeting, also, that you treat the teacher as a partner, not an adversary. This is essential if you wish to fully exploit the opportunity to help your child.

Parents and the teacher may well have different objectives in a meeting of this nature, but it is far from impossible to find common cause.

Your goal for the meeting is as follows:

The teacher should be familiarised with the advantages of new findings concerning your child's difficulties in reading and/or spelling. In cooperation with you, the teacher should motivate your child to keep going and allow them to hand in homework in typed form.

The teacher's goal is to look good in the eyes of parents and colleagues through the success of his pupils. The teacher also wants to have one problem less in the class – in this case your child!

Consequently, you both have an interest in your child overcoming their dyslexia. The only problem is that through this book *you* are now better informed than the teacher, therefore they may feel their authority is in danger (unless they have also read the book).

The core issue here is how to convince the teacher of the effectiveness of this concept without them losing face.

This goal can be achieved by employing the motivational dialogue described in the previous chapter. You should conduct a motivational analysis of your child's teacher for this purpose. In this case, it is vital, that you treat your child's teacher as an authority whose know-how you need for your common objectives. The meeting with the teacher should therefore take place on an equal footing.

How to identify the teacher's motives

Adults and, by extension, teachers are driven by the same motives as children, namely self-affirmation, social representation, self-fulfilment, social acceptance and security.

The social representation motive is of central importance for many teachers.

Teachers are very knowledgeable and wish to pass their knowledge on to anybody who will listen. Day in, day out, they stand in front of a class as a leadership personality. They seek – and need – respect and admiration. The teacher knows more than anyone else in the class and is also a specialist in dealing with awkward parents.

But does this also apply to your child's teacher? Which other motives are also important to them? Any comments your child has made over time about the behaviour of the teacher should be considered in order to make a rough estimation of his or her motivational profile prior to your meeting. I would therefore like to take this opportunity to illustrate a few wilfully exaggerated examples.

"Frau Schmid sang a song today and tap danced in front of the entire class! It was really great, Mama, and we all clapped!"

This happy soul teacher likes to demonstrate what she's good at in front of the class, even when it has nothing to do with the subject being learned, *and* she earns a round of applause! This is an indication that social representation is particularly important for her. She wants to be admired for that which she does and to enjoy a high-status level.

"Herr Schubert really went to town on Harald today. Harald kept causing disturbances as he was trying to explain to us how to do the math text exercises correctly. We then had to do the whole thing again until even Harald had understood it."

This teacher wants to achieve objectives he has set for himself. He measures himself against whether he reaches these goals or not. He wants to – and must – achieve self-affirmation. If, for example, he feels the achievement of these goals is jeopardised by the bad behaviour of a pupil, he reacts in an "aggressive" manner towards the child. Nevertheless, he doggedly pursues his goal until he has attained it. No doubt about it: this teacher is motivated by self-affirmation.

"Herr Bremer showed us creepy pictures from the plague during history today and told us lots about it and how awful it was for people back then. We also had to think up scenes and act them out. All the while he played strange music from that time in the background. Half the class was only messing about, but he didn't care less! He simply kept going with the children who wanted to continue."

This teacher is self-assured and works in a creative fashion, not letting a noisy classroom distract him in any way. He also does not suffer as a result. All this indicates that he is a "self-fulfiller". Chaos doesn't annoy him he's creative!

"Elisabeth pulled Theresa's hair and made her cry, but Frau Maier said nothing. You can do anything you want when she's in the class. She even asks us sometimes what *we'd* like to do!"

Frau Maier appears to be unsure of herself. She is just cannot deal forcefully enough with her pupils, even when it is really necessary – poor Lea! This obvious incompetence is visible to all: most of all to the children. All indicators point to a strong security motive. It is also possible that this teacher continually asks the school management when and how she should do things.

"Herr Reichelt said today that everybody had to read a passage from the reading primer, to which Robert said that we were all able to read ourselves without doing it out loud. Robert is so cheeky! But the teacher then said he was right and that everyone should read it alone for themselves.

This wasn't possible, because Jens then said that we could all read together out loud! Well! Then everybody started to argue with each other until Herr Reichelt said he could read it out himself. Even so, the boys continued to fool around even while he was reading!"

This teacher apparently always agrees with and repeats the arguments of others and strengthening them as a result. He then does just about everything to avoid conflict. No doubt that he is motivated by social acceptance.

You can compile a motivational analysis of this kind based on that which your child tells you and your previous experience with the teacher, and this in turn can serve as the basis for the meeting.

The motivational analysis for Herr Schubert results in the following profile: self-affirmation 70 %, social representation 60 %, self-fulfilment 15 %, social acceptance 50 %, security 30 %.

As you can see, success (self-affirmation) is important for this teacher so he always wants to achieve his self-set goals. Of secondary importance, but also significant is his need for recognition and admiration in the group (social representation). *Last but not least*, he also feels the need to be accepted (social acceptance).

The motivational dialogue is the method of choice here to fulfil these motives. As you already learnt in chapter 6, you need to take the structure of the dialogue and sequence of the meeting into consideration if you are going to gain the support of the person you are trying to win over (as planned) for your objectives.

The structure of the motivational dialogue is therefore the same: introduction – addressing the problem – finding a solution together – summary – success monitoring

Introduction: The Wrong Way

"Evening, Herr Schubert, so we meet once more, aha! We've got a number of problems to discuss with you again, so let's get right to the point."

The teacher is likely to be apprehensive if the introduction is as brusque and abrupt as this. Aside from this, the mention of the word "problems" means he is already looking for a way to protect himself. Consequently, a positive introduction is more to your advantage

Introduction: The Right Way

"Good evening Herr Schubert, great that we can meet up. We appreciate it; we know that teachers today have less and less time at their disposal!"

"It's my pleasure, Frau Wilhelm, Herr Wilhelm. Please take a seat."

"Before we come to the point, my husband and I would just like to say how much we enjoyed the forest walk with the ranger last week. Lars loved every minute of it, and he'd like to become a forest ranger himself! I was so pleased that you invited us parents to join in. Such a nice gesture Herr Schubert."

"Thank you, Frau Wilhelm, very nice of you to say so. Now, you asked for this meeting to talk about Lars ..."

You should always launch a dialogue in a positive manner, helped by a friendly, sincere greeting in *your* own style. Avoid any pretence.

To strengthen the positive atmosphere, you could cite an example and put the person you are talking to at the center of the meeting. The purpose of this meeting is to win the support of your child's teacher, which is why the lamplight should be on *them* and not your child or you.

Addressing the problem: The Wrong Way

"Why the hell have you given our Lars a 6 again?! The boy works his socks off and you just ignore his efforts completely. It's the school's fault that he has these problems with spelling – and your fault too! Do you always have to repeat the same thing time and again?"

If you subject the teacher to an all-out attack and blame them, they are almost sure to defend themselves. Addressing the problem in this negative manner only risks the teacher digging their heels in and refusing to liaise with you.

Any future cooperation with you, if any such occurs, will at best be only superficial in nature. They are hardly likely to welcome any new ideas and consequently, will in all likelihood not motivate your child to try a new method.

Addressing the problem: The Right Way

"Well, Herr Schubert, we have a problem, and we'd very much appreciate your help as a specialist. Lars was really crushed after the last dictation, because he had been practising for months on end and only managed a 6 again!"

"Yes, Herr Wilhelm, I'm also sorry about that. Lars is a nice, out-going boy. He really tries, and his marks are good in mathematics and the other subjects. But German just doesn't seem to be his forte."

As you can see, the situation is addressed as a mutual problem, considerably increasing the chance that the teacher will also see it in this light and not apportion the blame for it to your child or parents.

Reaction to statements or objections: The Wrong Way

.... But German just doesn't seem to be his forte...."

"Now go on, Herr Schubert, take a closer look at it, you see he's making a lot less mistakes, and not just this time round!"

There is a risk that the teacher may feel slighted as a result of this approach and feel the need to justify themselves, and this is definitely not good! They believe they are speaking from *experience*, but you have, so to speak, an *advantage in terms of specific knowledge*.

Reaction to statements or objections: The Right Way

"Maybe you're right, Herr Schubert. On the other hand, of late, Lars has been making enormous strides to the fore, and the average number of spelling mistakes he makes has dropped significantly. There were only 13 in his last spelling test, he was making 25 just four months ago!"

"Well, with so much work to correct, it's hard to remember everything. But, when you look at it this way, it really is a noticeable improvement. Hmm..."

"And it gets even better, Herr Schubert. Lars is reading his second book in three weeks, voluntarily," says Frau Wilhelm excitedly.

In the event of objections, react in a positive manner towards your converser. If possible, express your understanding for his position, using expressions such as:

"... maybe you're right ... I understand what you mean ... if I was in your position, perhaps I'd also think the same ...".

However, you should avoid reinforcing the point of view of the person you are debating with. Use *specific examples* to underline your position, as this may well encourage your interlocutor to make his own proposals for solving the problem:

"The historian Barbara Tuchman once said that books are windows on the world, Frau Wilhelm," says Herr Schubert thoughtfully.

"I'd very much like Lars to take part in the new course for dyslexia to accelerate this improvement. I think it would really do him good. This is a professional course based on the Reuter-Liehr method, and it's recommended by the German Association for Dyslexia and Dyscalculia.

Lars will be able to train as he wishes exclusively with syllables during the course. I think that's the key to success. What do you think? Should I register Lars for you?"

Reception of proposals: The Wrong Way

"BUT I've heard that the children don't improve very much at all using the syllable method. Look, read this book and you'll see why!"

The offer of help from the teacher is abruptly rebuffed. He feels his standing as a specialist is being questioned, consequently it will be extremely difficult to interest him in the book. Avoid saying "but", as it practically means "no"!

Positive reception of proposals: The Right Way

"Herr Schubert, many thanks for your offer of assistance, we really value your professional support."

Even if you are convinced that the teacher's proposal made will not contribute to solving the problem, he still deserves recognition for his suggestion.

Further argument: The Wrong Way

"Lars has improved, and he could get even better if you would only cooperate. Can't we tackle the problem together?!"

Rushing towards a solution without any consideration for the concerns of the teacher is a sure recipe for failure.

Further argument: The Right Way

"With regard to this situation, I'm sure you'll be interested to know how Lars has manage to improve so enormously in reading and spelling in a very short period. He breaks up the words in the same manner as employed in the syllable method but, instead of just syllables, he also reduces them to the individual letters, all with the aid of a computer keyboard. He copies texts every day by typing them from books," says Frau Wilhelm.

"And that's not all. He also imprints individual letters by playing alphabet games. Well, actually, we play these games with him regularly," adds her husband.

"Is that all?" asks Herr Schubert, rather astonished. "Most peculiar!"

Don't allow any surprise or scepticism on the part of the teacher to put you off. Refrain from reacting in an aggressive or defensive manner, providing evidence in a calm manner instead. Use the "if/then" approach when making your arguments. This is the best way to convince the teacher to cooperate with you.

Finding a solution together: The Wrong Way

"We can't just abandon Lars! He has to type his homework, and he must be allowed to hand it in in a typed format."

If you make *demands* of and try to force solutions on the teacher, they are automatically inclined to oppose you and endeavour to defend their authority. Moreover, it is inappropriate to place the emphasis solely on the advantages for your child. *The teacher* should remain the focus of your attention. In this case: why should they employ a method they have never heard of?

Finding a solution together: The Right Way

"Herr Schubert, it's just as we said – we need your help. You can well imagine the enormous effort required – depending on the day and situation – to convince Lars to complete all the typing exercises or alphabet games *and* do homework at the same time. We're sure as a specialist that you have some idea how we could combine the typing training and homework effectively. You've got to help us"

"Yes, well, if he has German vocabulary to do for homework, he may type this."

Leave it up to them initially to make proposals regarding solutions. You should use interrogative forms such as "Surely you have an idea?" or "You most probably have a suggestion….?" or similar for this purpose.

This allows you to support their motive of social representation and convince them to stand behind the solution **they** propose... Helping Lars to achieve better results improves the class average score. The teacher will look good in front of their colleagues. The manner in which you frame your request allows you to work towards manoeuvring their solution in the direction you desire.

Positive reception with further argumentation: if – then

"That's a big help! IF he could hand in his essays and *all* his homework in *typed* form, wherever possible of course, THEN he'd improve even quicker, which means one problem less for you Herr Schubert! And it would be even better if he could take his laptop to school and type as often as possible, instead of writing by hand. We would, of course, switch off the WLAN to stop him surfing in the internet during lessons," says Frau Wilhelm enthusiastically.

"I think that's all a little too much for me, Frau Wilhelm. It's a very unusual demand you're making of me. I can assure you that none of my colleagues are open to exceptional arrangements like these! I'd be the only one." Herr Schubert leans back slightly in his chair and folds his arms.

Dealing with resistance: The Wrong Way

"So, what? We're talking about the future of our child!"

Putting it like this suggests that you are indifferent to the teacher's position. You are placing the focus on *your child*, rather than them.

Dealing with resistance: The Right Way

"I can well appreciate your concern," replies Frau Wilhelm in an emphatic, yet relaxed tone, "and I respect it. Fact is, Lars is making 50 per cent fewer mistakes after only four months, and he's reading books now! If you can help us to help him continue in this way, then he'll get good marks in German for the first time in his life. He could get to higher secondary school with your help, Herr Schubert.

I'm sure you have a suggestion how we could organise this on a practical level. The homework aspect is only half the problem. We have nobody to turn to. We need you. And Lars needs you to praise him and encourage him to continue."

"Frau Wilhelm, let me make a suggestion. We'll give it a shot! I'll help Lars as well as I can. We'll let him type his homework for about a month – when and where it's suitable to do it this way. Should major problems arise during this time, Lars will have to write out his homework like all the other pupils. But if things work out well, he can thereafter bring his laptop to lessons," replied Herr Schubert.

Always express your understanding for your counterpart's position and employ the if/then technique when shaping your arguments. If, as in this example, the teacher declines to accept your proposed solution and, instead, makes a suggestion of their own (for a trial month) which will also achieve that same goal, then you should accept the proposal.

The second-best solution is always the better in cases like these, as the teacher can identify with it. The main thing is that your objective is achieved as a result. In the event of them having *no suggestions*, employ the proposal technique to reach a solution. Your proposals must be acceptable to them, fulfilling their motives and leading to your now mutual goal.

Summary: The Wrong Way

"Alright, then let's try it!"

Following every discussion, both parties should clearly understand what has been agreed upon.

Summary: The Right Way

"That's a good idea, Herr Schubert. You're right, this solution is sure to be more acceptable to your colleagues, and Lars won't have any unfair advantage over the other children. You'll be helping Lars to ensure his success, and you'll also raise the average mark of your class.

That's great, Herr Schubert! So, we're agreed that you will also enlighten Lars on the huge advantages this methodology brings and will continue to bring. We'll stick at it together! As of now, he can hand in his homework typed. Agreed?" tells/asks Frau Wilhelm.

"It can't hurt to try, I suppose," Herr Schubert replies slowly.

When summarising, clearly indicate what you have agreed to do. Once again, cite the advantages which the solution has for everyone involved and which correspond to the teacher's motives. Always round this off with "Okay?" or "Agreed?" This makes it more difficult for them to say "No" – provided, of course, that your proposal is reasonable and will lead to the goal being achieved.

Success monitoring: The Wrong Way

"Okay, that's how we'll do it. Well, goodbye until the next time!"

If you have not expressly agreed on when you will meet again, everyone involved is less motivated to keep to the agreement. In addition, should you then wish to discuss success or lack of it, without prior arrangement, it will immediately be considered a crisis meeting and taken as a bad omen.

Success monitoring: The Right Way

"Okay, let's let this thing run for a month and then meet here again in four weeks to discuss the success our efforts have achieved, alright?" says Frau Wilhelm. "In the meantime, Herr Schubert, may I suggest you take a look at this book? It describes the typing method. But I should warn you it's fascinating stuff, but unconventional. It would help us all so much if we were reading from the same page."

"Well, a breath of fresh air never did anyone any harm," smiles Herr Schubert. "Okay, Frau Wilhelm, thanks for the book. I'll tell you what I think of it in four weeks."

"We'd be very interested to hear your opinion of it, Herr Schubert. We'd also like to thank you very much for your understanding, and your support."

"Don't mention it, and we can discuss whether to continue this trial when we meet again. Frau Wilhelm and Herr Wilhelm, I hope you have a pleasant evening. Gute Nacht"

Success monitoring is used to check upon measures to ascertain whether they have been implemented as agreed. Simultaneously, it is also used to trace the level of success these measures have had to date.

Agreeing to success monitoring in advance will ensure that the next meeting is a constructive one. It provides an opportunity to ascertain what has improved and by how much so. It is also an opportunity to take pleasure in the success your child has achieved through your cooperation with their teacher and to increase motivation as a result. Alternatively, you can work on improvements for the future, without any apportioning of blame for what went amiss in the past.

Practise makes perfect

You can improve your chances of success by practising the motivational dialogue several times at home with your spouse or partner. You can also switch roles, with *you* playing the part of the teacher, then your spouse or partner. Assess these dialogues critically by examining what was good and what could be better. If possible, you should also ask a person you trust to observe your efforts and provide additional feedback.

Further situations in which you need to act and react in relation to the school

In the above example, the parents asked the teacher for a meeting to win over his support for the typing training concept. However, there are other difficult occasions such as you being asked to meet with the teacher to discuss your child's poor behaviour, or perhaps they feel excluded or even mobbed by classmates; or to discuss the possibility of your child repeating a school year voluntarily.

How to proceed if your child disrupts lessons.

Teachers frequently assume (and not always incorrectly) that the family home is responsible if a child behaves badly at school. However, *you* now know that everybody is predisposed by specific motives. We all *need* security, acceptance, recognition, self-affirmation and scope – to a lesser or greater degree – if we are to be creative.

Dyslexia and the constant failures associated with this mean that your child's motivational fulfilment is threatened to an extreme degree. Depending on their motivational disposition, your child can react with uncertainty, extreme attachment or aggression, or through bragging, boastfulness and acting the clown.

In the case of pro-actively motivated children in particular, this behaviour can become disruptive and have a dysfunctional influence in the family and at school. Our first instinctive reaction is to try and protect our child by warding off criticism from outside. However, if you are called into the school because of your child's disruptive behaviour, you should employ the *"positive take-up"* technique resolutely

- Demonstrate understanding for the difficulties the teacher has in coping with your child.

- Welcome the opportunity to cooperate with the school in order to influence your child's behaviour in a positive manner. Should you have similar difficulties with your child at home, show no reticence and openly admit this, explaining that you are working together with your child to get these under control.

- *Cite examples where your child has improved in reading and spelling. Your child may make fewer spelling mistakes or read somewhat more fluently now and with greater enthusiasm.*

- Develop measures together with your teacher which could lead to an improvement in behaviour.

- Justify your suspicion that this behaviour is related *to lack of success* in school. Show the teacher that you are using the *Kennedy Concept* in dealing with and overcoming this challenge.

If no improvements are yet evident, explain to the teacher how you are working on the problem at home. At this point, you could try to win the teacher's support for the line of reasoning illustrated above in the case of the Wilhelm family, namely that your child is motivated and wishes to continue typing and playing alphabet games – and that their efforts deserve some recognition.

Promote the idea of your child handing in homework in typed form. Don't despair if this does not work. *Keep going until you achieve success!* However, do insist on an agreement on monitoring your child's progress where the accomplishment of the agreed measures is discussed again after a week or a month. This allows you to demonstrate just how seriously you take the teacher's concerns and your child's education.

How to proceed if your child is insecure and/or in danger of becoming an outsider

It unfortunately lies in the nature of things that defensively-oriented children are sometimes intentionally excluded by other children. These increasingly isolated children often react to failure with tears and distress. They fear unpractised dictation and class work, often experience difficulties going to sleep and, indeed, sleep poorly and not infrequently suffer from somnambulism (sleepwalking).

They complain of headaches and stomach pains, particularly prior to a test. Some of their schoolmates react to this with increased rejection and exclusion; the risk of mobbing rises and often the child suffers from depression as a result.

Attentive and socially aware teachers are often mindful of what's going on in their class and with the children, take the initiative and approach the parents in order to find a solution.

However, teachers are frequently so busy that they fail to pay specific attention to children who do *not* disturb lessons. They fail to notice their difficulties or place them further down their list of priorities. In such cases it is up to you as a parent to grasp the initiative and seek a meeting with the teacher.

I also recommend in this case that you proceed as described in our example with the Wilhelm family. Additionally, you could follow this by encouraging proposals from the teacher as to how, overall, your child's behaviour and conduct in general in the class could be improved. *I recommend that you seek specialist advice outside the school if there is any suspicion of depression.*

In the case of a defensively motivated child, it is essential that you and the teacher offer them more *security*. The purpose of your conversation with the teacher is to be able to tell your child: "We've spoken to your class teacher, and he wants to help you to improve. He'll speak with the other children so that you get on better together, without mentioning your name."

In the case of mobbing, the teacher may still remain inactive *after* your meeting, simply because they do not know what to do about it. You should approach the school management in this case.

What you can do if you notice that the school is working with unsuitable methods

You notice that your child is reading poorly and their spelling is even worse, but nothing is really being done to correct this at school. (This "method" is quite widespread in Germany) In fact, your child is even *permitted* to make numerous spelling mistakes. Your child is perhaps learning according to an initial sound table and with *complete* words which it is permitted to combine independently. Mistakes such as "tmahto" for the word "tomato" are not corrected. No unpractised dictations are written. The main concern for you is that your child will memorise these errors – which most certainly is the case. Fortunately, this "method" is slowly dying out in Germany.

Let us take another example. While learning the alphabet, your child simultaneously practises *syllables*. This makes it more difficult for your child to imprint each individual letter with the depth and permanency needed.

We are now navigating dangerous waters surrounded by treacherous reefs! If your child is immediately confronted with syllables and words in the first grade, or is allowed to write the words at their discretion, as a dyslexic they will have little chance to imprint individual letters to the required depth.

Additionally, it is highly probable that a child that is a borderline case will tip towards, and in this instance, develop full-blown dyslexia.

Your chances of helping your child through a motivational dialogue with the teacher in such a situation are extremely poor! After all, the teacher is convinced that their teaching methods are best, otherwise they would not employ them! Even when the prerequisites are so unfavourable, it is still worth a try.

As always, you should try everything to win the teacher's support in achieving your goals. *Do not criticise the methods employed by the school.* Instead, you should emphasis the creative aspect of our (and your) new method when addressing the problem and the (potential) advantages for the teacher If the school focuses strongly on using the syllable method from the outset, emphasise the educational rigour of this methodology.

Continue to argue that you *also* want to support these efforts, and this would be possible if your child could hand up his work in a typed format. Do not "ask", but rather suggest that it be used as an additional aid complementing the efforts of the teacher.

In order to avoid any dispute over methods, you should refrain from saying that you work with the *Kennedy Concept*. You can mention this eventually after your child has overcome its dyslexia. However, the teacher may then try to take the credit for the successes achieved.

Should you let your child repeat a class or not?

Many parents feel that their child is completely overwhelmed in school and give consideration to repeating a class. This can be a major advantage for a child with dyslexia, as they have the chance to *catch up* through typing training and alphabet games without trailing behind when faced with increasingly difficult workload.

After all, these requirements are intended for children who do *not* have dyslexia. If you notice that your child is completely overstretched, then repeating a class should be given serious consideration. Some parents even ensure that their child drop down a class during the school year.

If you wish to take action (which I recommend), a decision of this nature requires careful consideration:

- Repeating a class is *advisable* if your child is overburdened *in every respect* by the consequences of dyslexia.

- Your child has no command of the basic rules of English, and both you and your child feel overburdened in general.

- They are also achieving poor results in mathematics and other subjects, despite the fact that they try very hard in school and at home

- You should also give consideration to the degree of social development. Dyslexic children not infrequently appear to be one or two (or more) years younger in terms of their behaviour. This "childishness" occurs because dyslexia can be part of a general *developmental delay*. Frequently, it is the appropriate stage of social behaviour that is less advanced in this context.

Where these criteria apply to your child, downgrading by a class will have more positive than negative consequences. Your child will no longer feel overstressed and can make up for their dyslexia through typing and playing alphabet games. They may initially miss their friends from the old class, but they can still meet them during the break and after school. Your child will make *new* friends in the new class and also have the time to play with them.

Also: your child has the opportunity to develop at their own rate.

Repeating a class is *inadvisable* if, with the exception of the subject English, your child's performance is good. Numeracy is intact, and grades in other subjects are acceptable. Your child not only understands the material, but is also interested in other things to a degree commensurate with their age. In addition, it fits in well with the class. Your child is independent and, apart from its problems with reading and/or spelling, has very few difficulties.

Following your own assessment of the situation, you then need to convince your child and the teacher.

How to behave if you want your child to repeat a class, but the teacher does not agree

Many teachers are against repeating because they have *numerous* children in the class who are dyslexic (they just don't know it). Why should an exception be made for *your* child? Your child will miss its classmates, and this will increase their feeling of uncertainty. Moreover, teachers frequently also argue that the problem will sort itself out in time.

Do not be unsettled by these arguments. In reality, cases where the reading and writing center of the brain and consequently, the reading and writing skills of a child mature *on their own* are more the exception than the rule. *Do not depend on it.* You need facts and examples in this situation to back up your arguments for repeating a class:

"Imagine, Frau Kluge, Michael and I needed *one* whole hour yesterday to write the essay, followed by 40 minutes for the text exercises in mathematics. He needed to re-read the text on the rainforest several times before he understood it correctly. In total, he needed two hours and 20 minutes for his homework. And this happens almost every week. According to the Education Act in North Rhine-Westphalia, 60 minutes are reserved for homework in the third class.

We're both worn out, and something has to change. We need your help! **If** Michael could repeat a class, it would relieve him of a lot of pressure. **Then** he'd be able to do his homework and his typing exercises without becoming so exhausted and upset so very often. He'd learn how to spell properly and, overall, he'd improve at school. That is what we both want"

You can convince the teacher and school management of the benefits of repeating a class if you are at all times receptive to their objections, whilst reinforcing your position according to the if/then principle.

Now what does your child have to say in this matter?

How to convince your child that repeating a class is necessary

Children usually do not like to repeat a class as, quite simply, they want to be with their friends. Your child also wants to save face and not risk being considered inferior or being called stupid by others. You should also employ a motivational dialogue in this situation. Show understanding for your child's objections without reinforcing them, and continue to push your argument forward with "if/then":

"**If** you repeat, it'll be easier for you and **then** you'll get better marks for reading and writing over time. You will be able to keep up with the others in class. Wouldn't that be nice for you?!"

Be resolute and continue in pointing out further advantages:

"Typing training and alphabet games will help you overcome your problems, once and for all! Then you'll be one of the *best* pupils in your class, and no longer among the worst. Wouldn't that be even better!"

"I know you'd like to stay with your friends, look: you can see them during the break *and* play with them *after* school. And do you know why? Because you'll have more time for yourself and won't need to spend long hours doing your homework.

Also, you'll meet a lot of nice kids in the new class, so in the end you'll have even more friends than now."

Remain unswerving, try to keep things on an even keel. Making excessive demands of your child will not help. (This may lead your child to refuse to type and play alphabet games because they are exhausted – and what would you do then?)

Children generally grow used to their new class after about three weeks.

How to react if the class teacher wants your child to repeat a class, but you don't

Demonstrate understanding for the teacher's arguments by receiving them positively. If they indicate good reasons (such as we outlined above) as to why your child should repeat, then agree with him!

Otherwise, demonstrate using examples and *facts* why your child is good enough for their present class, particularly if they only perform poorly in English, but exhibits few problems in other subjects. Attest to the progress your child has already made in English due to typing regularly. This is positive evidence that your child will improve further and that repeating a class is unnecessary. Point out that your child will be discouraged if, despite all these achievements, they still have to repeat.

After explaining your position, try to arrange a trial period for your child to remain in their class and an appointment for a second meeting to review your child's situation.

What you can do if the teacher rejects the "letter method" of the *Kennedy Concept* and refuses to cooperate with you

You will find some teachers impossible to convince, either because they are completely swayed by another method, or they find the letter method too unconventional or too simple. These teachers may also be fundamentally opposed to any proposals made by parents and regard these as an attack on their authority, or they may be so overworked that they have little energy left to additionally motivate your child or allow for any exceptional arrangements.

Avoid any conflict with these teachers and "take cover" instead. Give in to the teacher's demands. Homework should then be handed in in handwritten form. However, it is not necessary for the teacher to know that your child typed it *beforehand* and then copied it in handwriting. Just you take sole charge of motivating your child!

Meanwhile, everything will continue in school as the teacher wishes. At home, you and your child should continue working meticulously applying the *Kennedy Concept*, and you will savour the moment even more when you can surprise such a teacher with the successful results.

You now have a few options which will help you navigate your family vessel safely past the dangerous reefs of dyslexia and school and arrive safely in the harbour of literacy. Just hold the tiller firmly and, together with your crew, steer adeptly towards your destination! Go for it!

I could almost end my book here if it wasn't for one other problem ..., namely, if dyslexia were not so often accompanied by dyscalculia and attention deficit hyperactivity disorder (ADHD). I would like to address both these disabilities in the next two chapters and give you an insight on how they come about and how to deal with them effectively.

8.   Five and six ... are nine?

Dyslexia and dyscalculia

"For goodness' sake, Lea! Four from 12 is 8! You *know* that, we've been practising subtraction the whole week! Now try and concentrate – we've already spent two hours doing this!"

Lea had been practising letters for months, and her reading and writing had really improved. However, the same could not be said of mathematics.

"But Mama, I really am trying!" Lea screamed back. "Can't I play with Hannah now?!" She burst into tears, crying uncontrollably.

Her mother back her own tears but, when she was alone, she sobbed as exasperation and a feeling of helplessness overcame her. "I really don't know what's happening here. Maybe dyslexia also occurs in mathematics!"

It never rains but it pours

Lea's mother is right. There really is a condition similar to dyslexia which is encountered in relation to mathematics. The term used for this is *dyscalculia*, and it frequently occurs *in addition to* dyslexia. My experience indicates that about 33 per cent of children with dyslexia also have dyscalculia. Dyscalculia is frequently overlooked, given that dyslexia is more noticeable and that better results can be achieved in mathematics through practising and memorising.

As with dyslexia, dyscalculia can occur in a weaker or more pronounced form, with children suffering from a more distinctive dyscalculia experiencing major difficulties right from the very first class. These children find it almost impossible to comprehend the numbers one to 10 in the first few weeks. For example, a child is unable to calculate $2 + 3 = 5$ with any reliability and fails to identify the correlation with $5 - 3 = 2$. At the other end of the spectrum, children manage to achieve *good* results over a longer period if they practise repeatedly at home to iron out any perceived "careless mistakes" which are, in reality, calculation errors. This strategy succeeds until the demands made on them increase. A child suffering from dyscalculia typically develops major problems with fractions at a later stage as the demands made on their mental calculating capacity become even more abstract. Despite this, very many children with dyscalculia manage to get through secondary school right up to about the seventh or eighth class before a calculator is no longer of help and expensive additional tuition becomes a necessity – if the money is there.

Many parents try to suppress or downplay this problem with comments such as "Well, my child's marks are better in maths than in German" (or in your case, English dear reader). However, this only means that your child is compensating for their dyscalculia through greater diligence and application. The dyscalculia may, of course, not be as pronounced as their dyslexia.

Warning Signs

Should you notice that your child needs an inordinate length of time for arithmetic during homework and makes numerous "careless mistakes", you should consider the possibility that dyscalculia is "in play."

Many our parents at the Kennedy-Schule say that they need to dedicate a lot of time to helping their children at home, repeatedly practising the four fundamental arithmetic operations (+ - x ÷) according to the same singular pattern. This strategy produces acceptable results for as long as the same sequence is employed. For example, let us assume that as usual, your child needs to complete a series of addition exercises, followed by subtraction problems and, finally, exercises involving multiplication.

Major problems then arise if these exercises are no longer tackled in this sequence. If, for example, these exercises are assigned in a mixed order during class work and, additionally, some are in text form to test flexible thinking, your child with dyscalculia will probably fail. This is particularly the case where mental arithmetic is involved.

The greater the demands on flexibility and abstract mathematical ability during this type of exercise, the greater the difficulty your child will experience when trying to compensate for an arithmetical disability through learning by heart.

These difficulties are possible indications of dyscalculia, but they are not automatically a sign that your child is actually suffering from this condition. However, they are reason enough for you to examine these phenomena more closely.

Why dyscalculia frequently remains undetected

Primary school teachers are not trained to recognise dyscalculia. Therefore, many who have not been informed of this condition or lack any further professional training in this respect tend to assume that your child is not intelligent enough to understand basic arithmetic.

The majority of teachers then recommend that parents practise more with their children at home "until they get the hang of it". Indeed, this can help to a certain degree – through rote learning. However, my practical experience shows that learning by rote (memorising) does not achieve any enduring success in the case of a child with dyscalculia, *when they must calculate using mental arithmetic only.*

Your child is incapable of retaining these rules or implementing them in full. They make mistakes, a great number of mistakes. A vicious circle begins: arithmetic exercises are practised – your child makes lots of mistakes – endless repetition follows to eliminate these mistakes – your child reacts with despondency and/or defiance ... Anxious parents are unsettled and unsure as to whether these problems might actually be a reflection of the child's level of intelligence, or whether they are incapable of concentrating or simply going through a rebellious phase. For the uninitiated, it is indeed difficult to differentiate between cause and effect in this vicious downward spiral.

Another factor which may disguise dyscalculia is the modern calculator. It is designed for higher-level mathematics in secondary school, enabling pupils to enter mathematical problems and obtain the correct solutions. A prerequisite for this is the inputting of exact information in the right order.

Indeed, a good teacher engaged for additional tuition can easily show pupils how to do this. The only certainty here is that these intelligent pupils will not be able to *mentally* compute effectively, despite sitting mathematics in their final school examination!

A further difficulty in diagnosing dyscalculia is the fact that dyslexia on its own often leads to major problems in arithmetic. Dyslexic children frequently fail to identify numbers and arithmetic operators with any degree of reliability, often writing them down incorrectly. They may also transpose digits in many cases, examples being 56 instead of 65 or 235 instead of 532, etc. Their arithmetic calculation is then correct, but using the wrong numbers means that the results are invariably incorrect.

These children also have major difficulties when it comes to properly identifying the operators for addition (+), subtraction (–), multiplication (x) and division (÷). Naturally enough, dyslexia also plays a role here, as it can lead to significant problems when it comes to text exercises.

So how do you determine whether your child's difficulties with arithmetic are the result of dyslexia or dyscalculia?

If your child has a reading disability but, apart from possible difficulties with text exercises, transposed digits and confused arithmetic signs, is good at arithmetic calculations, their difficulties can be traced back to their dyslexia.

If your child is poor at arithmetic but reads well, the cause of their difficulties can then be found in dyscalculia. The probability that both conditions exist is high if your child's performance is poor in both reading *and* arithmetic (as described in this book).

Consequences of a failure to identify dyscalculia

If a child has difficulties in the first year with the number range from one to 10 and simultaneously, suffers from dyslexia (which is not always the case), here in Germany they are deemed a candidate for a special needs school for children with learning difficulties. Intelligence tests sometimes appear to confirm this classification – if the *wrong* tests are applied.

We still receive reports from parents who believe that an intelligence test examines reading, writing and arithmetic. In the case of children with dyslexia and dyscalculia, only the results of the *non-verbal* part of this test are valid. The danger being that children with learning disabilities with normal to high intelligence would be classified as less gifted and sent to special needs schools.

How a child in this situation feels is barely imaginable. They are filled with doubts about their own ability probably thinking they are stupid and, essentially, good for nothing. After all, they have received official confirmation in black and white that they are not intelligent. Depending on temperament, a child in this situation may react with resignation and accept their fate, or their frustration in school may lead them to seek recognition in other areas. This need can lead to unruly behaviour, drinking and drug abuse in extreme cases, and a descent into delinquency and crime cannot be ruled out.

For the majority of children with dyscalculia who are allowed to remain at a regular school, the daily schedule is an uninterrupted regime of very hard work – for both child and parents. The greater the demands encountered in mathematics, the more time you need to invest to ensure that your child fully grasps the material involved. That which has already been learnt needs to be continually revised, and exhausted mothers repeatedly tell us that they need to start again from the beginning the very next day.

It is not unusual for the father to pick up where the mother has just left off and continue labouring with the child when he comes home from work. Very soon, the entire family is at its wits' end, and all because the child is incapable of doing their homework alone. The consequences are additional stress and conflict – and a very unhappy child. Naturally enough, mathematics is even less fun under these circumstances. Children are filled with doubts concerning their ability, and uncertainty grows alongside a feeling of inferiority. This can be alleviated to a certain extent when the school is supportive and caring.

It is not difficult to imagine other consequences which this situation harbours, as your child is continually under stress and feels queasy and unwell. Sleep disturbances, nausea before school and a drop in general performance when it comes to school work are sadly the norm, as this vicious circle spirals further out of control.

The fact of the matter is, that the child is incapable of realising its full potential and, in addition to jeopardising their future career prospects, their personal development is also at risk. As an adult, dealing with figures on a daily basis is difficult and, indeed, frequently very embarrassing. Examining financial matters, making decisions about the purchase of a car or house and investments are all obstacles where there is a justifiable fear of making major mistakes.

Arguments are a frequent occurrence in the family of children affected by dyscalculia, simply because they take so long to do their mathematics homework. A rift in the entire family is practically inevitable, and the parents' marriage is frequently strained as a result. As nobody knows what is wrong with the child, the problem soon shifts from the actual situation and is personalised:

- "His teacher is moving too quickly. Tim simply needs a little longer to grasp the material being taught."

- "We never had problems like this in our family, they must come from you!"

- "You just show too little patience with Anna. Shouting at her is not going to help! She came running to me as soon as I came home. What on earth are you doing with her all day?"

Last but not least, the daily practise with your *Kennedy Concept* for overcoming your child's dyslexia is also put at risk. How are you supposed to play alphabet games or type for 20 minutes every day if you are labouring over mathematical problems for hours on end?

Practical experience has shown me that the integrity of the family threatens to unravel if parents cannot master this challenge. *Do not despair, together we will prevail!*

So how exactly do you determine whether your child has dyscalculia?

Criteria for identifying dyscalculia

Your child needs too much time and makes too many mistakes

The demand for tuition in mathematics is by far the greatest for any subject in the *Kennedy-Schule*. All pupils have to sit an entrance test which consists of questions on the four basic arithmetic operations in the number range from one to 100. Practically all the pupils take too long at this (up to 10 minutes in individual cases) and often make 12 mistakes or more in a test consisting of 25 tasks. This includes advanced-level secondary school pupils who are studying to go to university. (At school in Germany, mathematics is always a compulsory subject).

The very same occurs during class. Addition and subtraction, multiplication and division are calculated mentally with the greatest of difficulty – and often little success. Your child can achieve passable results if it has enough time at its disposal. Where this is not the case, the number of "careless mistakes" increases considerably, these being in reality arithmetical errors, and a poor mark is often the only reward for a child under (time) pressure.

If a child makes more than 12 mistakes in a test consisting of 25 simple arithmetic exercises (so, half or more being incorrectly answered) and needs more than seven minutes, it is highly probable that they are suffering from dyscalculia.

Your child uses its fingers as an aid to counting

"Fabian, you must be able to add nine and four without using your fingers! You're in third class now. And apart from that, your teacher told you not to do that! You have to calculate it in your head now. Okay, how much is nine plus four?"

"Ehmm, just a minute ... twelve, Mama."

"No, no, no! Look, you've got a nine, so just take one from four and add it to it. Now, how much is that?"

"Ten"

"Exactly, and how much of the four do you have left now?"

"Three."

"Very good, that's right. And what is three plus ten?

"Eh, thirteen, Mama."

"You see? You *can* do it without your fingers! Let's try it again, this time with no fingers. Okay, how much is eight plus seven?"

"Thirteen?"

If your child uses their fingers regularly to count and still does so *after* the first class, you should take into consideration that your child has dyscalculia. This behaviour indicates that your child has difficulties with abstract numbers and arithmetic per se, and needs concrete objects to illustrate the task (fingers in this case).

Incidentally, "finger counters" are not only restricted to primary school level. There are enough pupils in the eighth grade (in Germany age 13 -14) who still count on their fingers.

Mental arithmetic demands great effort and is defective

Mental arithmetic is, in a manner of speaking, the litmus test for your child's numeracy, as it exclusively involves abstract thought. Even children who suffer from concentration disorders are capable of mental arithmetic if the prerequisites for arithmetic are given. In extreme cases of attention deficiencies, your child can, depending on how they feel, perform well when solving mixed arithmetic problems. Some even excel at mathematics. However, this is impossible in the case of dyscalculia.

A gradation can be applied in this respect to arithmetic tasks which cause difficulties for children tormented by dyscalculia. Following lots of regular practise, they can also generally solve addition exercises in their heads with a *relatively* high degree of reliability. However, 'careless mistakes' which, in reality, are arithmetical errors are encountered time and again.

Subtraction exercises require greater effort, being more abstract. Your child can achieve good results on paper when they have enough time, but the level of performance is often considerably poorer when it comes to mental arithmetic.

Exercises involving multiplication can be challenging, and children with dyscalculia almost always fare badly when faced with mental tasks involving division. As always, your child performs better with a lot of practice, using a pen and paper and having adequate time to complete the exercises. Problems always arise when they have to calculate for division in their head, and this is compounded by the unsuitability of fingers as an aid.

Last but not least? these children often fail when it comes to doing fractions. The level of abstraction involving fractions is even greater, and the fact that they involve addition, subtraction and multiplication often overwhelms these children. The introduction of fractions from the fifth class onwards (in Germany) requires that a child is competent in dealing with the four basic arithmetic operations.

In addition to this, again in Germany, children are not yet allowed to use a calculator until the seventh grade. Please note: your child's failure to understand the *arithmetic process* is not always the problem. Indeed, the numerous arithmetic mistakes they make, increasing uncertainty and the resulting confusion are the factors that condemn a child to failure when dealing with fractions. Again: it is not their ability to understand the mathematical process involved.

Failure in transitional exercises involving the 10 and 100 thresholds

Not all children with dyscalculia count on their fingers. Many endeavour to use mental arithmetic and succeed to a greater or lesser degree, depending on the severity of their disability and the amount of time at their disposal.

These children can cope to an adequate degree when working in the lower number range, but difficulties arise, as always, when abstract demands increase. Many children can cope to a greater or lesser degree with exceeding of 10 (say, 5 + 6) by counting on their fingers or through mental arithmetic, despite the significant additional effort involved in this process.

The difficulties arise if your child needs to calculate up to and over 100. Mistakes typical of exercises of this nature include 8 + 8, 19 + 7, 23 + 9 or 77 − 14. Your child can conceal these difficulties on paper if you "train" them regularly and intensively prior to class work, but they may well forget how to do these problems two days later. Forcing your child to calculate these type of transitional addition exercises mentally is almost always a recipe for failure.

Difficulties with multiplication tables

Many children suffering from dyscalculia, but not all, cannot retain multiplication tables. Parents, let your child write out and memorise a multiplication table from one to 10, then develop a question-and-answer game from this which can include practical examples. "Look, Maria, this bag contains six apples. How many bags do I need to buy for our family if I need 18 apples?"

Both the parents and child make enormous efforts to memorise multiplication tables through continuous repetition – but it is all in vain. Typically, after two weeks the process has to be repeated.

However, not all children suffering from dyscalculia find it difficult to retain multiplication tables. Many can recite every row mechanically right up to 10 x 10 – but only *mechanically*! It is highly probable that a talented parrot could also manage this task. Children are unable to *apply* this knowledge flexibly and fluently, and division in particular leads to major difficulties.

Major difficulties with text exercises

Children with dyscalculia tend to fail when it comes to text exercises. Having learnt the solutions of standard calculations by heart, they then try to apply these according to a fixed pattern. This strategy is suddenly thwarted when they need to solve questions in a text format and endeavour to decide what is being asked and what needs to be calculated.

The order of individual components in the problem is hardly recognisable. What exactly should be calculated, and how should this be done? A child who has achieved good results in standard exercises but fails in text exercises is clearly exhibiting signs of dyscalculia, if you can rule out a reading disability.

Your child cannot work independently

"Mama, how do you do this?" – This is a question heard all over the country and probably the entire world! Children continually ask their parents to help with arithmetic because they just cannot cope on their own. And as your child does not have the prerequisites for this task, you as a parent need to provide assistance. Day in, day out.

"My child suffers from dyscalculia – what can I do?"

Practising for hours on end with your child is precisely what you should *not* do

It is essential that you change your approach and jettison all the old practices! Any attempt to improve your child's numeracy through continuous repetition of the four basic arithmetic operations and multiplication tables is in the long run, doomed to failure from the outset.

Help of this nature may require you to invest hours of your time and, in a vain attempt to finish early, you ultimately end up giving your child the solutions to the problems. We continually hear from exhausted parents seeking support that they do exactly this.

This 'assistance' simply offers your child repeated confirmation of their inability to do arithmetic as it should be done. Your child also sees clearly that other children are better without help. As a result, your child becomes unsettled and doubts their own ability. They believe they are stupid and, as I have already described, react with everything from tears and resignation to depression, defiance, aggression or buffoonery. This enormous investment of time in mathematics homework and the associated failures can then lead to major upset and discord in the family.

Our search for the best solution

On determining that children at our *Kennedy Tutorial School* were not improving to any noticeable degree in arithmetic, we reduced the size of groups from six pupils to three. The didactic principles underlying our efforts were:

- the stimulation of attention to the task at hand

- familiarisation with problem-solving techniques

  and

- the promotion of working independently.

The ulterior motive behind this was the premise that each child had their own very individual problems with mathematics. Therefore, each child and teacher had more time in the smaller group to solve these difficulties on an individual level. We then trained the four basic arithmetic operations with the children during tuition, followed by mathematical topics which were being covered at school. We then allowed each child practise these extensively.

The method achieved a degree of success where the pupil was allowed to continue practising without interruption right up to the school test. Once they stopped practicing so intensively (two 90-minute sessions every week) performance dropped dramatically.

One special case springs readily to mind. The boy in question, whom I will call Peter, was experiencing major difficulties, and a transfer to a special needs school for children with learning disabilities seemed inevitable in the near future if his performance in arithmetic did not improve.

We were simultaneously working with our dyslexia concept to improve Peter's performance in German. Peter was receiving individual assistance in mathematics from a primary teacher who worked intensively and extremely conscientiously with him, but to no avail. Despite all these efforts, Peter was sent to the special needs school. The conventional approach of providing additional tuition in mathematics to familiarise Peter with numbers and arithmetical processes had failed in his case.

Nevertheless, I thought, an understanding of numbers is unquestionably of significant importance and, indeed, a prerequisite for learning mathematics! As with *letters* in the case of dyslexia, *numbers* should be imprinted through the senses of sight, hearing and touch by children suffering from *dyscalculia*.

So we got down to work and introduced arithmetic games into our lessons. The children played with colourful pictures, game templates and number cubes. Fractions and percentage calculations were illustrated using media such as the segments of a circle. The children employed the same principle to assemble geometric shapes. Numbers themselves were taken apart and reassembled, added, subtracted, multiplied and divided in a playful manner. Flashcards were used in an attempt to help the children learn their multiplication tables.

The children played and played with numbers and the four basic arithmetic operations, visibly enjoying this form of "tuition" very much indeed. Parents supported our efforts and were relieved to see that their offspring was finally having fun with maths.

Results achieved at the proper school improved somewhat, but unfortunately still left a lot to be desired! The "harvest" was disappointing, even though we had taken apart, combined and reassembled numbers in a descriptive and playful manner with the children. When the children stopped attending extra tuition at our school, their results deteriorated either immediately or by degrees. Again, it seemed that the children had failed to gain a firm grasp of numbers.

The causes of dyscalculia

I continued my research, once again consulting Dr Held's paper on the developmental phases of childhood. Motor skills, speech and the ability to read and write are all biological functions whose efficiency depends on the maturity of the individual brain region responsible for the execution of the specific activity.

We knew that, in the case of dyslexia, that the brain's reading and writing center needs to be continually fed with the simplest unit of writing (that is letters) through the senses of sight, hearing and touch if this region is to develop and mature completely.

The real problem associated with dyscalculia is similar to that encountered in relation to dyslexia: numerous mistakes – despite the child's improved knowledge! It therefore stands to reason that dyscalculia must also relate to immaturity of the center for computation in the brain. The next question was obvious.

> If tackling numbers in itself cannot ensure numeracy, what exactly is *behind* the numbers? The answer: quantities!
>
> A specific *quantity* is to be found behind every number (or, more precisely, every digit), and this value is an abstract representation of this quantity.

Having thought this through, I was convinced we were on the right track. The next question I posed addressed the failure of children with dyscalculia to relate to abstract numbers which, depending on the culture involved, are illustrated by a variety of symbols. The Romans used a capital X to represent the number 10.

So: associating the figures 1 and 0 with the quantity 10 is by no means obvious or self-evident. This connection must first be established in a child's brain. In other words: The prerequisite for establishing this connection is that center for computation has to be biologically mature!

Matters become extremely difficult for these children if playing or working with quantities is only sporadically addressed or, indeed, never offered in the first class. In this case a child with pronounced dyscalculia is immediately at a grave disadvantage. A clear indication of this is the instinctive tendency of these children to use their fingers as an aid when transforming abstract numbers sequentially into quantities. This enables them to count correctly.

Dyscalculia: Cause and Resolution

A biologically "immature" center for computation in the brain is underdeveloped. This functional weakness prevents it from linking *quantities* to abstract *numbers*. The numerous arithmetic mistakes made by these children reflect the severity of this immaturity.

Conclusion: The calculating center of the child's brain will only mature if it is fed with individual quantities via the senses of sight, hearing and touch. Children will only learn to calculate without continually making mistakes subsequent to this brain region maturing. In other words, tuition should consist exclusively of quantity counting games.

The solution: games linking quantities with numerals

"Thinking techniques" are of no help, as the problem results from a lack of maturity of the brain's center for computation. A "curative" educational method is required that employs suitable materials which ensure that children can count and calculate in the entire number range from one to 100.

We therefore introduced quantity games such as Ludo to lessons. When it came to the four basic arithmetic operations, the children had to count the quantity in each case, repeating this continually. The response was extremely good, as all the children seemed to instinctively sense that these games could help them. We also introduced many other games which involved the children linking quantities to numbers using all their senses.

The results achieved were immensely gratifying for us, the children and their parents, because the children were finally able to *learn arithmetic properly*. Even after dyscalculia training ended at the *Kennedy Tutorial School*, the children continued to perform very well over an extended period of time. Many of them managed to make it to lower and even higher-level secondary schools. It is not unusual for former pupils to register their children with us for the same course(s).

How children can practise games with quantities

The approach is very easy – for both you and your child. You merely have to allow your child to count freely selected quantities up to one hundred. You can also do this in the form of a game, using dice as in, for example, Ludo. If, for example, your child throws a six, it moves its token forward six squares, counting as it does so: 1, 2, 3, 4, 5, 6. But what happens during this? Let's slow things down and take a closer look at the procedure, step by step.

Sight

On throwing a six, your child *visually* registers the six dots on the dice. These impulses are transmitted via the visual center to the center for numerical calculations where they are memorised.

Touch

Allow your child to count the six dots on the dice by running their index finger over them. They will also memorise these in the calculating center via the motor function. Quite a few children cannot visually memorise and recognise the six dots in a single attempt, so counting the individual dots is necessary. When your child then moves their token on six squares, counting these individually as they do so, the motor-center of the brain transmits these six impulses to the center for computation where they are then memorised and over time *imprinted*.

Sound

When your child counts 1, 2, 3, 4, 5, 6 out loud the six separate sound impulses are transferred via the center for hearing onto the center for computation

In other words, you are ensuring that your child *imprints* the quantity six completely over time using the senses of sight, hearing and touch *and* then links this automatically to the name of the number symbol – which is six in this case.

Please note that this memorising process is not a passive procedure. These impulses stimulate the brain cells, leading to stimulation of the synapses (nerve endings). These in turn then develop and grow further according to the (genetic) extent intended by nature until, eventually, the brain center matures fully.

All other participants profit whilst playing. They also memorise the six via their sense of sight and hearing – not of touch because it's not their turn. But they also see the dots on the dice and the six moves on the board, and they hear the numbers one to six when they are called out individually by another player.

The game Yahtzee also ensures that your child repeatedly sees quantities and can count also using his finger, out loud.

On the other hand, Monopoly is less useful in this regard and should be avoided. Although children play with dice and tokens, much of the game also involves paper banknotes. A one-hundred-dollar note (or any other currency) is just *one* banknote that represents the abstract value of 100. It is best to put this game to one side for the moment, as there is a definite risk of slipping from concrete counting into abstract symbols. *Beware!* This will only divert you from concentrating on the quantities that your child desperately needs!

The crucial point here is to achieve targeted stimulation of the brain center for computation via the senses until this center (biologically) matures. Perhaps the better term for dyscalculia is the scientific one: *Developmental Dyscalculia*.

As with dyslexia, your child should practise for *20 minutes every day without exception*. The reward for this effort is that your child can carry out the four basic arithmetic combinations reliably and independently; and do his or her homework without your help. This we know.

Your child can also imprint quantities *without* a board game and dice, practising arithmetic in a wholly *concrete* fashion.

Exercises and games with pebbles for counting up to 100

In order to do this, you will need a quantity of pebbles, buttons or Lego bricks. Only quantities are counted here – nothing else.

This means that your child should lay down the appropriate quantity of pebbles in horizontal rows and groups, and in rows and columns for multiplication and division, all the while calling out the names of the numbers.

They place the pebbles together or *divide* the groups for every arithmetic operation, speaking out the names of the numbers during this. This anchors the respective quantities firmly in the brain via the senses, namely sight, hearing and touch.

A few examples clearly demonstrate how this works. In these, each x represents a pebble, Lego brick or button.

1.   Addition 4 + 9:

xxxx + xxxxxxxxx = 13

Your child should therefore add 9 pebbles to the 4.

2.   Subtraction 15 – 8:

xxxxx xxxxx xxxxx – xxxxx xxx = 7

Your child should subtract 8 pebbles from the 15 with his hand.

3.   Multiplication 4 x 3:

xxxx xxxx xxxx = 12

4.   Multiplication rows (for example multiplication table for 5):

xxxxx

xxxxx xxxxx

xxxxx xxxxx xxxxx

In this example, have your child place pebbles representing the multiplication table for 5 from the one to the 10, each row below the other – as shown above.

After completion, ask questions such as, what is 3 x 5?

- ✓ Allow your child to count rows one to three first (from top to bottom)
- ✓ And in the third row then count from left to right.

5. **Division 15 ÷ 3**

xxxxxxxxxxxxxxx

Your child counts out 15 pebbles then forms three groups from this quantity, each consisting of five pebbles:

xxxxx   xxxxx   xxxxx

A tip for you: Always have your child form *rows of 10* if they need to lay down the answer to addition tasks. This will make crossing the ten's boundary visible. For example, take 19 + 5. The solution is then as follows:

xxxxxxxxxx

xxxxxxxxxx

xxxx

You can enhance the attractiveness of this quantity exercise further if you use gummy bears or jelly babies – which your child can then eat at the end of the 20-minute exercise time!

Combine this exercise over and again with the other games. Continue practising multiplication tables like this until your child knows these by heart, and alternate between laying quantities and learning by rote. The emphasis should always be on *laying out* quantities.

How to introduce quantity games and exercises

Understandably enough, you may face some resistance from your child during this process. The older your child is, the more they will feel compromised. After all, no child likes to hear that they need to start right from the beginning again and count quantities with their index finger every day!

React in a positive manner to any objections:

"I know you think these exercises are for babies. But the goal is to imprint the *quantities* behind the numbers even deeper and more firmly in your memory-bank. This has nothing to do with your intelligence or your age. If you play these games regularly, you'll be able to count well and you'll get better marks! Come on, we can do it together. Let's get started!"

This style of reasoning is particularly effective with pro-actively motivated children. Another approach should be adopted for defensively motivated kids:

"You Know, Claire, you're like a beautiful tree – the problem is that your roots are just not growing down deep enough into the soil. These games and exercises will help your math-roots grow better and anchor you deeper in the earth, then you'll reach up to the heavens and be covered in pretty blossoms, just the way your spirit is meant to be."

Our experience shows that your child will cooperate if you and your family are all committed to this approach.

How to master your child's dyslexia and dyscalculia at home

You will need to practise for 20 minutes every day laying quantities and linking these to numbers to achieve good results. Together with typing training and alphabet games, this means 40 minutes at least five times a week (daily is optimal). This may sound like a lot, but the pay-off is that *you can save time* elsewhere.

Up until now, maths homework has meant you spending a lot of time laboriously "solving" problems together with your child. Despite this, your child continually fails to grasp the subject, so really the whole exercise is a waste of time, entirely ineffective and frustrating for all involved. Or: your child learns by rote and, as soon as they stop, down go the grades!

The best approach is to show your child how to solve the problems right at the beginning of homework! They then write down the solutions, or copy *your* solutions which *you* have arrived at in *discussion* with your child. This allows you to kill *three* birds with the same stone. Firstly, the homework is done and the teacher is happy. Secondly, you gain time to do the quantity and alphabet exercises and, thirdly, your child has time to play afterwards.

Find out if a regulation relating to "equalisation of advantage" for dyscalculia applies where you live and, if so, request that it be applied to your child at school. This rule ensures that caution is exercised when assessing marks for your child in mathematics if a school transfer is being considered.

Contact the school and try to convince the teacher through a motivational dialogue to use this method for your child so that he can support you and urge your child to continue with quantity games and exercises at home.

How you know your child is improving

In the case of severely pronounced dyscalculia, children frequently cannot identify the six dots on a dice in a single attempt. However, their ability to achieve this improves increasingly over time. We have also observed that children who always use their fingers to count gradually desist from relying on this aid, simply because their ability to do mental arithmetic improves.

Their success at crossing the "tens boundary" becomes increasingly better, even where higher numbers are involved.

The number of mistakes is a sure indication. The number made usually decreases small step by step and, also over time, they become increasingly confident in using multiplication tables. While reliably retaining and reciting sequences, they also know how to apply tables correctly, including for division and calculating fractions.

Last but not least, children improve at solving text exercises (provided they do not suffer from a reading disability).

But this (developmental) training requires time and, as with dyslexia, children should practise regularly for at least a year. Our experience shows that initial improvements are evident after four weeks. It is important for both you and your child that you take note of even the slightest progress and point this out to your child.

"Mama, I got a 6 again in mathematics!"

"That's a pity, you've been working so hard lately. But it's not all bad. Look, you solved the first two problems correctly. Well done!! You'll see that if you keep at it things will get even better!"

9. "Why is my child so inattentive?"

Dyslexia and attention deficit

"What do you mean, Mama?"

"You know, I'm beginning to ask *myself* the same question. I asked you to get two bottles of mineral water from the cellar a quarter of an hour ago - and here you are sitting at Daddy's workbench and tinkering around! What are you doing with the sandpaper and scissors?"

"Making butterflies."

"But it just doesn't fit together!"

"Yes, it does, Mama. Look, it works when I do it like this."

"Hmm, so it does, well done. Oh, now you're distracting me! Take these two bottles to your Daddy at once."

"Yeah, okay."

"Who should you bring them to?"

"Daddy."

"Who?"

"Daddy!"

"That's right, now run along – and make sure you *do* go to Daddy! Here's me running around after you all day to make sure you get things done!"

"Thanks, Mama, that's kind of you!"

"Oh, get out!!"

The parent's dilemma

The dilemma faced by parents of inattentive children

Some parents despair completely when faced with the chronic inattentiveness and forgetfulness of their children while, at the same time, often wondering just how well their child can focus on a task when it seemingly wants to. This is well reflected in the example of Emilia making her sandpaper butterflies!

If this scene is familiar to you, your child could also suffer from an attention deficit in addition to its dyslexia. If so, it certainly would not be alone in this respect. Many children suffer from dyslexia *and* have great difficulty directing their attention.

We all know that children are *naturally* unpredictable at times and tend to follow their hearts when it comes to doing things, sometimes failing to adhere to the rules and acting in a manner that goes beyond accepted norms. They forget agreements or drive their parents to the brink of a nervous breakdown with their fidgeting. This is normal to a certain degree.

However, there are also children who all too often deviate from the norm and get into trouble as a result. They seem incapable of breaking out of their absent-mindedness and high spirits. If this behaviour is encountered at such a blatant level, it may well be that chronically poor concentration is the cause of the problem. This is also known as attention-deficit hyperactivity disorder (ADHD).

Alarm signals

By and large, parents of such children tend to notice that their child is easily distracted - *frequently*. Indications of this include fidgeting at the dinner table and getting up and running to the window if someone passes. Your child finds it difficult to concentrate and focus on the task in hand. When it comes to cleaning their room, your child is often willing to do this but cannot finish the task, being continually distracted by the things they find.

A child with an attention deficit often exhibits little endurance when it comes to everyday tasks such as preparing their school bag properly for the next day in school. When you try to talk to your child about these things, they suddenly begin to tell you about the neighbour's dog! Many of these children have difficulties when it comes to organising tasks and activities, simply because their attentiveness fails them. As a consequence, games and activities that they want to do with others often never take place.

The affected child frequently fails to carry out instructions completely and is forgetful in everyday activities, not knowing what homework they have to do and often losing and mislaying school things and other objects. As a parent, you are constantly reminding your child what to do, admonishing them when they forget or do something wrong and ensuring that their behaviour does not cause too much trouble. Discussions with educators, teachers, other parents and neighbours regarding this behaviour are more the norm than the exception.

It is the inattentiveness which troubles so many parents. It is particularly frustrating when your child appears not to be listening, and a generous dose of patience and understanding is required here! Inattentiveness can occasionally lead to your child endangering themselves. For example, on a visit to the swimming pool, you tell your child to stay with you in the changing room until you have dressed but, as soon as you turn your back, your child is gone and getting ready to jump into the deep end of the pool, even though they cannot swim!

Things become really exhausting if an attention deficit is further complicated by hyperactivity. Your child is constantly restless, frequently fidgets with their hands or feet, is unable to remain still and spreads restlessness and irritation among others. They find it difficult to play quietly and are often "on the go from morning to evening".

Your child behaves as if they are driven by an inner engine to be in a constant state of motion (and, in fact, this is indeed the case). This behaviour can extend to bedtime, as these children often find it hard to go to sleep and are very restless the whole night through. Many wake up at night and are afraid. In addition to being exhausted trying to keep up with their children, parents are also astonished by what they can achieve, be it in a sporting, musical, technical or other creative areas!

The actions and behaviour of a child apparently "driven" in this manner are the main features of hyperactivity. In addition, babbling and effervescent chatter is also frequently observed. Your child comes home, throws their school bag and jacket down somewhere – having left their hat in school and, naturally enough, their homework – and tells you in, so to speak, a *single* breath about an argument between two children during the break, what the teachers did or did not do and how stupidly the caretaker was dressed ...! After relating this tale for ten minutes without a break, they suddenly walk away and start to play with their robot. Two minutes before lunch, your child suddenly grabs their bike and cheerfully cycles off ....

These children may have a hard time in school. Despite their (often) high intelligence, they have difficulties following lessons and observing the rules at school. They are continually distracted. If a classmate drops a pencil on the floor, your child turns around immediately. These children can have enormous problems when it comes to just sitting quietly, and they not infrequently disturb other children through the constant unrest they spread. "Can you lend me your pencil? I've forgotten mine." – "What kind of a pencil case is that? Where'd you get it?" – "I'll borrow a copybook from Thomas." – "I want to see what those men outside are doing." – "Frau Kübler, I lost a shoe during the break!"

In addition, they fail to complete tasks and – as described above – forget to write down their homework or do not even *realise* that they have homework assignments on a given day!

Inattention and hyperactivity are often associated with impulsiveness. These children act *immediately* without thinking and have difficulty waiting until it is their turn to do something. They often blurt out answers in the classroom, despite not being asked by the teacher. An impulsive child tends to interrupt and disturb others, trying to impress them while, at the same time, acting the clown in class. Telling such a child to be quiet is often ineffective, because these children do not really have themselves under control.

If such a child is confronted concerning its behaviour, they will try to deny their difficulties in order to save face and because they do not understand why they act this way. Impulsive children act without thinking, running across the street without first looking both ways. They are constantly involved in conflicts because they interfere with and rub people up the wrong way, cause unrest and put themselves at risk.

There are two different types of ADHD, but mixed forms are also encountered. In addition to the robust, hyperactive and impulsive case, a quiet, dreamy and sensitive type of child also exists. This second variant without hyperactivity is frequently referred to as ADD (attention deficit disorder). The children affected are often extremely sensitive. At the slightest rebuke, they burst into tears and run off crying, or they counter attack and reproach their parents, often with tears in their eyes.

These (dreamy) children are so sensitive that many parents feel they can only be handled with kid gloves. Parents modify their own behaviour, compensating in as far as possible to accommodate their child and trying to deal with their sensitive offspring in an even more diplomatic and considerate fashion.

They often have the impression that their child's emotional development has been delayed by one or even two years. ADD children appear childish when playing with other children, are poor losers and complain a lot if they do. They feel rejected if their friends react adversely and, in fact, are easily pushed to the edge of the group.

Such children not infrequently slip into depression.

Strong mood fluctuations are a typical side effect encountered in ADHD and ADD: your child is day dreaming happily one moment, but totally devastated the next. The hyperactive child often experiences alternating phases of enthusiastic activity with aggressive outbreaks followed by total exhaustion.

If you have a child with dyslexia, it may also suffer from ADHD without you having yet recognised this. It has become evident in our school that dyslexic children and adolescents suffer more frequently from ADHD than one thinks. The ADHD has remained undetected in the majority of these cases.

Why ADHD frequently remains undetected

Detection is difficult because many doctors, specialists and educators regard the behaviour of a baby or child as normal during the developmental stages of a pre-schooler. Many ADHD babies cry a lot at night (and during the day). Indeed, in many cases, this behaviour is practically uninterrupted, so parents instinctively take the baby or toddler into bed with them. This pattern may continue for several years, with the parents' actions often being interpreted as a *cause* of the child's poor sleeping behaviour rather than a *reaction* to the child's indisposition and malaise.

Some of these babies even show signs of extreme restlessness on the changing table. Many parents think, "Well, it's just high spirits. My husband and I are also pretty high spirited!"

Parents may not have the opportunity to compare their child with others. It is quite natural for them to regard their own child's behaviour as normal and adapt to it. If it cries a lot, the parents think this is just "baby being baby". If it is unfocused and easily distracted, this is regarded as being a little exuberant and undisciplined. After all, boys will be boys, and, these days, girls are likely to be just as lively!

In the case of the "dreamers" who are typically uncertain and immature and tend to react very sensitively to criticism, parents adapt their style of upbringing to cushion the child's sensitivities, promote their talents and strengthen their self-confidence.

The restless type of behaviour becomes even more conspicuous when children participate in activities *outside* the family (such as children's gymnastics). The contrast to the behaviour of other children becomes clearer in this situation. Parents tell us that, due to an inability to stick to the rules, their children are often banished to the bench for not paying attention.

Parents are often questioned by the trainer about their children's behaviour. Mothers are also addressed again in the nursery or kindergarten regarding their child's lack of discipline. In other words, trainers, childcare providers and, later, schoolteachers simply consider these children to be badly brought up.

Parents are also frequently reproached by relatives because the children are deemed spoilt, too lively and come up with the craziest of ideas. Does this sound familiar to you?

Some parents vehemently reject this interpretation and ignore the behaviour of their child, while others go to the greatest of lengths to wean the child from their disturbing behaviour, with the parents' efforts frequently being rewarded by failure and they themselves being left feeling helpless.

This is especially true when it comes to hyperactive children. "Dreamers" are far less conspicuous. If they are noticed at all, they are classified as "followers" and considered harmless and not to be taken seriously.

The problems will only continue to grow if ADHD is not recognised and treated. Hyperactivity and impulsiveness can lead to aggression, because the children do not have their own behaviour under control and frequently do not even register or misunderstand the non-verbal and verbal signals of their playmates and teachers. These children have no bad intentions and often come from loving, friendly families. In the case of the dreamers among them, there is danger that they may shut themselves off even more, be ignored by their classmates and teachers and drift into depression because they are unhappy about their condition. It is therefore important to check carefully to ascertain whether your child has ADHD or not.

How to recognise ADHD

Only an experienced specialist is capable of reliably identifying ADHD, as they can conduct sound, systematic tests. However, you need a well-founded suspicion if you wish to consult such a doctor. An orientation test exists for this purpose which is based on the guidelines of the DSM IV (*Diagnostic and Statistical Manual of Mental Disorders*). It has proven to be a useful indicator under practical circumstances for detecting ADHD in children. A series of descriptions in this test allows you to estimate the degree to which they apply to your child. This helps you to determine if your child has perhaps ADHD and the severity of the disorder.

It is best to conduct the test three times, simply because your estimation is purely subjective. You should then print out the results which appear most objective to you and take them to the specialist.

For further information search the web using children with add and adhd. These sites is also considered to be very helpful:
http://www.chadd.org/
https://www.adhdfoundation.org.uk/information/parents/

ADS/ADHS orientation test

To complete the test, tick off only *one* feature in each case.

Short attention span – poor concentration (I)

My child is easily distracted
O Never   O Rarely   O Sometimes   O Very often

My child has trouble paying attention
O Never   O Rarely   O Sometimes   O Very often

My child rarely completes one activity before moving to the next
O Never   O Rarely   O Sometimes   O Very often

My child forgets that which it has learnt
O Never   O Rarely   O Sometimes   O Very often

My child makes many careless mistakes during school work
O Never   O Rarely   O Sometimes   O Very often

My child appears not to listen, even when spoken to directly
O Never   O Rarely   O Sometimes   O Very often

My child frequently finds it difficult to organise tasks and activities
O Never   O Rarely   O Sometimes   O Very often

Short attention span – poor concentration (II)

My child has no endurance (when it comes to everyday things)

O Never   O Rarely   O Sometimes   O Very often

My child suddenly talks about other things
O Never   O Rarely   O Sometimes   O Very often

My child frequently fails to carry out the instructions of others completely
O Never   O Rarely   O Sometimes   O Very often

My child does not know which homework it should do
O Never   O Rarely   O Sometimes   O Very often

My child frequently loses or mislays objects
O Never   O Rarely   O Sometimes   O Very often

My child is frequently forgetful during everyday tasks
O Never   O Rarely   O Sometimes   O Very often

My child switches abruptly from one task to the other
O Never   O Rarely   O Sometimes   O Very often

Hyperactivity

My child frequently fidgets with its hands or feet
O Never   O Rarely   O Sometimes   O Very often

My child cannot sit still
O Never   O Rarely   O Sometimes   O Very often

My child is a cause of unrest
O Never   O Rarely   O Sometimes   O Very often

My child is a cause of irritation
O Never   O Rarely   O Sometimes   O Very often

My child frequently finds it difficult to play quietly
O Never   O Rarely   O Sometimes   O Very often

My child is frequently "on the go"
O Never   O Rarely   O Sometimes   O Very often

My child frequently acts as if "driven by a motor"
O Never   O Rarely   O Sometimes   O Very often

My child talks excessively
O Never   O Rarely   O Sometimes   O Very often

Impulsiveness

My child frequently blurts out answers
O Never   O Rarely   O Sometimes   O Very often

My child denies having difficulties
O Never   O Rarely   O Sometimes   O Very often

My child finds it hard to wait until it is his/her turn
O Never   O Rarely   O Sometimes   O Very often

My child interrupts and disturbs others
O Never   O Rarely   O Sometimes   O Very often

My child shows off and acts the clown in school
O Never   O Rarely   O Sometimes   O Very often

My child is constantly involved in conflicts
O Never   O Rarely   O Sometimes   O Very often

My child acts without thinking
O Never   O Rarely   O Sometimes   O Very often

My child runs off without thinking
O Never   O Rarely   O Sometimes   O Very often

Sensitivity, possible depression

My child has strongly fluctuating moods
O Never   O Rarely   O Sometimes   O Very often

My child is easily hurt and reacts angrily
O Never   O Rarely   O Sometimes   O Very often

My child is *extremely* sensitive to criticism
O Never   O Rarely   O Sometimes   O Very often

My child is quick to cry
O Never   O Rarely   O Sometimes   O Very often

My child is a bad loser
O Never   O Rarely   O Sometimes   O Very often

My child has very little self-esteem
O Never   O Rarely   O Sometimes   O Very often

My child is despondent to the point of being depressed
O Never   O Rarely   O Sometimes   O Very often

My child seems to be more childish, less mature
O Never   O Rarely   O Sometimes   O Very often

The test is evaluated as follows:

If you come to the conclusion that the statements relating to your child are predominantly categorised under *sometimes to very often*, I recommend that you consult an experienced ADHD specialist.

ADHD test – advantages and disadvantages

A good ADHD test such as the above, provides you with the orientation you need, preparing you for a visit to a specialist and allowing you to present your reasons for suspecting ADHD in your child. These recognition criteria are sober and impersonal, having been developed by medical professionals. *You can and should cite examples of your child's behaviour during the meeting which match respective recognition criteria.*

The disadvantage is that all these assessments are subjective. What is "normal" in childhood or adolescence, and what not? The aim is to leave the realm of the subjective and to move up into that of the objective, and this is achieved by comparing your child with as many of their peers as possible. You should also list feedback from relatives, friends and educators that enables further objectification. The expert can then make a clearer diagnosis based on so much relevant information.

Other possible causes of poor concentration

You should also have a general practitioner check whether your child's poor concentration has completely different root-causes to that of ADHD. There are a number of illnesses and deficiencies that can cause similar symptoms.

Even if your child has little or no attention deficits, it makes sense to have them examined. This is a necessary step, both for the welfare of your child and overcoming their dyslexia.

Low blood pressure

Hypotension, a condition characterised by low blood pressure, can be identified through a simple medical examination. The aforementioned neurologist and child psychiatrist, Dr Fritz Held explained it as follows:

Hypotension occurs during childhood where a familial disposition prevails or as a concomitant symptom of a physical growth spurt. It is afforded too little attention because its symptoms are confused from the outset with a neurosis or even laziness. Hypotonic blood pressure can simulate a whole arsenal of neurotic symptoms:

- Fatigue, listlessness
- Dysphoria (general dissatisfaction) tending towards irritated aggression or depression
- Headaches
- Stomach aches
- Sleep disorders
- Concentration weakness
- Lack of performance

Hypotonic blood pressure is primarily responsible for typical restlessness while sitting which involves instinctive purposeful movements. The muscular pumping effect associated with these cause blood which has sunk to the lower half of the body to be pumped upwards again, thus preventing deficient blood circulation in the brain. This is the reason why hypotonic children enjoy playing games of movement. When seated for long periods at school or during homework, they exhibit the symptoms listed above which were then incorrectly interpreted as laziness, but were in fact caused by the act of sitting itself.

Iodine deficiency

Too little thyroid hormone is produced if there is a deficiency of iodine. The thyroid gland then enlarges in order to distribute the iodine (which is not available in sufficient quantities) as efficiently as possible. Iodine deficiency is determined by a medical examination. External identifiers are:

- Indisposition/malaise
- Feeling of fatigue
- Lack of concentration

- Listlessness to a complete slowdown
- Feeling cold
- Scaly skin
- Shaggy hair
- Circulation disorders

A child suffering from iodine deficiency behaves rather passively and exhibits certain traits associated with depression. It literally does not feel comfortable in its own skin. This condition can usually be remedied by administering iodine tablets.

Iron deficiency

Iron plays an important role in the formation of blood and transmission of oxygen. Fatigue and a pale facial colour are typical symptoms of iron deficiency. External identifiers are:

- Poor concentration
- Fatigue
- Slack, listless behaviour
- Brittle nails and hair
- Hair loss
- Dry or pale skin
- Cracks at the corners of the mouth
- Feeling weak and panting under stress

Your child may be suffering from iron deficiency without exhibiting the above symptoms. These detection criteria do not apply to an *incipient* iron deficiency, given that the deficiency is still subliminal. A medical examination will also provide reassurance and clarity in this case.

Zinc deficiency

Zinc deficiency symptoms manifest themselves in increased incidences of allergic reactions, chronic exhaustion, lack of drive, brittle nails with white spots, hair loss and depression. Night blindness and dry eyes can also be experienced.

Zinc regulates cell growth, cell differentiation and the structure of cell membranes. It is therefore involved in all immune functions and is responsible for strengthening the immune system

Medical institutes recommend a daily zinc intake of 12–15 mg. Optimum use of zinc in the body is achieved in combination with histidine, an endogenous amino acid. A side effect of this compound with histidine is its anti-inflammatory properties, and the body's biological toleration of it is three times greater than that exhibited for pure zinc salt. Zinc-histidine preparations are available without a prescription from doctors and pharmacies (in Germany)

Poor eyesight

Our experience has shown that dyslexia and visual impairments can indeed go hand in hand. If your child cannot see the letters of a text correctly, they are not stored optimally in the brain. I therefore always recommend that the child's vision be examined.

In addition to ordinary impaired vision, a particular impairment of sight has also been discovered where it is assumed that the adjustment of the eye lenses is incorrect. This phenomenon is called accommodation impairment. The *International Association for Binocular Vision* has stated that this heterophoria can be remedied by the use of prism glasses (measuring and correction methodology according to Hans-Joachim Haase). (Sources: International Association for Binocular Vision.

Internet: https://www.ivbs.org/information-in-english/

Hearing difficulties

I also recommend having your child's hearing checked. Do not be surprised if the results fail to show *any* hearing impairment! Bear in mind that, although your child can hear well, they may not be able to process the phonetic sounds of letters due to the immaturity of the brain's reading and writing centre. In a manner of speaking, the cause of this specific hearing impairment is to be found at this higher level.

Cause of ADHD: Immaturity of the area of the brain area responsible for the direction and maintenance of attention

Attention regulation is a biological function of the brain, and the two frontal lobes are the pertinent areas for this function. This network is supplied with neurotransmitters as "chemical" messengers through which information is passed on from one nerve cell to the next. Scientists currently consider ADHD sufferers to be victims of an impairment of this function.

Let me explain: A transmitting nerve cell typically emits the neurotransmitter-messenger required to pass information to the next cell. The remaining neurotransmitters are reabsorbed by the transmitting cell after the information is transmitted.

In the case of ADHD, however, the neurotransmitters are reabsorbed so quickly by the transmitting cell that the receiving nerve cell does not have enough time to record the information. This leads to an actual lack of "steering-material" in the brain, with attentiveness and motor skills being particularly affected. Since ADHD is caused by inadequate transmission of neurotransmitters in the brain, attempts to remedy this deficit need to have a measurable *positive* neurological effect.

Complete *biological maturity* of this brain region is the *prerequisite* for the child's ability to control and direct attention and its social behaviour.

When we look at ADHD from the point of view of innate child development, it becomes clear what the learning disabilities, dyslexia and dyscalculia, have in common with ADHD. Delayed maturation of the functionality of the respective brain center is a typical manifestation in childhood. *These disabilities may occur individually or in combination.*

What can you do about ADHD?

What can you do to counter your child's poor concentration? There are some methods that are proven to work, others that seem to work for *some* children but less for others, and other methods that are frequently recommended but are *not* effective and can even be harmful

1.   Ineffective methods

Homeopathy

Homeopathy is a controversial alternative method of healing. Surprisingly or, in fact, astonishingly, reports of success in the treatment of ADHD children with homeopathic remedies are repeatedly received. I say astonishingly because, according to the definition, no trace of the original active ingredient should remain in remedies prescribed! Opinions are divided here among orthodox medical practitioners on the one hand and naturopathic practitioners (naturopaths) on the other. Having said this, anything that really helps ADHD children in the long term should be considered as a possible remedy.

It is, of course, always beneficial if the affected child *believes* that they can concentrate better by taking a remedy. In fact (and studies have shown this time and again), in cases where homeopathic preparations are taken and a firm belief in the efficacy of this therapy exists, neurotransmitters are released in the brain, and this can lead to an easing of the symptoms. This phenomenon is known as a placebo effect.

My personal view regarding the efficacy of homeopathy is that in reality, homeopathic preparations do not contain any stimulants (apart from the sugars that make up the globules)

and therefore, do not activate any metabolic process in the brain. A placebo effect is all well and good, but if you really want to overcome your child's ADHD, an active approach is called for, not a passive one.

Aphanizomenon flos-aquae (AFA or blue-green algae)

In Germany, both the Federal Institute for Drugs and Medical Devices (*Bundesinstitut für Arzneimittel und Medizinprodukte*, BfArM) and the former Federal Institute for Consumer Health Protection and Veterinary Medicine (*Bundesinstitut für gesundheitlichen Verbraucherschutz und Veterinärmedizin*, BgVV) warn against taking AFA algae because there is no scientific evidence that they can be helpful when it comes to ADHD. In fact, they can even be harmful to health! In 2002, the Federal Institute for Risk Assessment in German (*Bundesamt für Risikobewertung*) wrote:

"So-called AFA algae, also commonly referred to as blue or blue-green algae, are cyanobacteria (*Aphanizomenon flos-aquae*). It is known that certain strains of these organisms form toxins that can attack and damage the nervous system."

Occupational therapy

Although many paediatricians prescribe occupational therapy, it appears to be more an attempt to soothe the mothers of restless children with an attention deficit than the children themselves. If children have difficulties with fine motor skills, this approach to treatment can be very helpful, but otherwise it is of little use.

Only activation of the brain metabolism at the synaptic gap can lead to an improvement in attentiveness. This stimulation must be targeted specifically at this brain region. Occupational therapy measures are too general in nature to induce the desired activation in the long term.

Psychotherapy

Psychotherapy attempts to treat the *effects* of ADHD on your child and, through therapy, to address the reactions of their environment to this condition, especially those of the parents.

The cause of ADHD is often sought in the manner of upbringing and personality structure of the people involved, rather than seeing it as the effect of a biological developmental delay in attention maintenance *in your child* with all its negative consequences for your child and the family.

2.　　Promising methods that achieve *partial* success

Successes are achieved in the following three methods, but it is unclear to what extent they can be *universally* successful in everyday life. They lead to stimulation of the brain, and activation of the brain metabolism is assumed.

Concentration exercises

"Lukas, concentrate on the candle flame for three minutes, then you can go and play."

Three minutes later: "Well done, we'll do it again tomorrow!"

Doing concentrating exercises with your child is a step in the right direction, as this exertion triggers an increase in the dopamine and serotonin neurotransmitters. This is exactly what your child's brain needs to strengthen their attention. However, the effectiveness of this approach depends on the intensity and regularity of training. This method is arduous and requires a great deal of discipline and perseverance. It can take years to achieve useful results – if at all.

Taking omega-3 and omega-6 fatty acids

The daily intake of omega-3 fatty acid can alleviate hyperactivity – or at least these are the findings of the Oxford-Durham study conducted with 117 children. These results are supported by those achieved in a study conducted at the University of Adelaide with 132 ADHD children (the Adelaide Study). The effectiveness of omega-3 and omega-6 fatty acids is attributed to the positive impact of these substances on the functionality of the nervous system and brain. A further study at Oxford University (2012) showed that signs of hyperactivity and defiance lessened when omega-3 fatty acids were taken and that many children could learn to read better. It remains to be seen whether these encouraging results can be reinforced by further studies and experience garnered from everyday life.

Biofeedback

With biofeedback, your child's body signals are converted into images and sounds via sensors attached to the body and ultimately displayed as images on a computer. Your child is given a mirror image of their condition, enabling them to influence their body and mind in a manner which is probably otherwise only achievable through in-depth meditation. Positive changes in body functions are amplified through feedback on the computer.

To achieve this, your child places sensors (two small sensor plates which measure the electrical resistance of the skin) on their fingers. Measurement results are forwarded to the biofeedback device connected to your PC. A reliable device provides you with exact information on even the slightest changes in skin resistance. Even minimum relaxation or tensioning is noticeable as a result. Skin resistance measurements enable the conversion of your child's body signals and their integration in controllable children's games by the program.

For example, let's take a look at a *balloon game*. A meadow is shown on the PC screen, with a mountain landscape in the background. Suddenly, a colourful balloon appears on the screen. Using the power of thought, your child must try to land the balloon on the meadow. Your child needs to relax deeply to achieve this and, depending on how relaxed they are, their body's signals cause the balloon to descend ... or ascend. If your child concentrates very hard on relaxing, the balloon descends. However, should their concentration lapse or ifthey become excited, the blood flows away from their fingers toward the brain, which releases adrenaline, and beta waves are produced instead of alpha or theta waves; the balloon flies away.

Your child must try to train their concentration and attention so that they can achieve a state of deep relaxation. At the same time, they try to perform well by gaining more points in games than their last attempt or by outplaying their playmates. Good biofeedback products offer a variety of games and playing variations whereby the level of difficulty and sensitivity of measurements can be varied.

The findings of Dr Ulrike Leins' scientific investigations at the University of Tübingen in Germany have tended to underline the effectiveness of playful neurofeedback applications with children. According to Dr Leins, training with these devices achieves results which, if not better, are just as positive as those achieved through treatment with medicine.

I must admit that I don't find this conclusion particularly surprising! After all, the ultimate goal is stimulation of the brain to animate its metabolism. Self-stimulation of your child– encouraged by the ambition to win the game – probably releases the appropriate neurotransmitters your child needs to remain calm and concentrated, and it may also be assumed that brain maturation is simultaneously activated.

Advantages of biofeedback games:

Families can spare themselves the stress of introducing and administering a course of medication. The games are completely devoid of any side effects and can be played together with others or alone. The results are measurable (namely how deep and well your child can relax). Acceptance among teachers, educators and other experts is generally greater than for medication. Children can play at home, and the games are relatively easy to integrate into day-to-day family life.

Disadvantages of and difficulties relating to biofeedback games:

Solid scientific evidence (and some very positive feedback for our mail-order department creative learning, *crealern.de*) exists to support the benefits of these games, but not to the same extent as is available for treatment with drugs. Scientific opinions are not yet unanimous with regard to the scientific relevance of these positive results.

As with all curative education measures aimed at maturation of a particular brain region, children need to practise these regularly. *Repetition* is what counts! These exercises must be scheduled parallel to typing exercises, alphabet games and, where appropriate, arithmetic games. This is eminently achievable if you take a determined and planned approach and win over the school's support.

Unfortunately, more than a few children tend to cheat to achieve better results. The sensors can be manipulated by pressing actions. If your child is inclined to fool about, you should always remain present for as long as they are playing.

3. Methods that have been proven to work in the long term

Medication

The most well-known medications to have achieved this effect under practical conditions and in numerous studies over the last few decades are *Ritalin, Equasym* and *Medikinet*. All of these contain the active substance methylphenidate, and there are now several other medicines and active ingredients of this kind available on the market.

Less familiar, but perhaps more benign in its action, is *Piracetam* which Dr Held used for many years in his practice. With regard to the biochemistry of *Piracetam* (and, indeed, the effect of this group of stimulants), he writes the following in his treatise on "Drug-Supported Brain Maturation Therapy in Childhood and Adolescence" (*Der Kinderarzt*, Volume 15, 1984, No. 8) As far as I can ascertain recent studies show similar improvements in maturation.

https://www.healthline.com/nutrition/piracetam#section2

"If we consider biological maturation to a level of appropriate functioning to be a specific brain function of childhood and adolescence, and if medications exist which physiologically activate the brain metabolism, it is consistent that maturation can be activated in this way. Biochemical studies on animals indicate an improvement in the energy potential of the brain cell achieved through a faster ATP turnover. *Piracetam* increases the rate of incorporation of radioactively labelled phosphate into cerebral organic phosphate compounds and stimulates the metabolism of phospholipids and nucleic acids (Giurgea, Gobert). The increase in neuronal protein formation was determined indirectly through the increase in polysomes, the protein synthesising devices of the nerve cell (Burnotte). *Piracetam* therefore promotes the metabolism of the brain, an indispensable prerequisite for the undisrupted execution of all brain functions."

In the same issue of *Der Kinderarzt*, Dr Held also points to the positive effect of *Piracetam*, not only in the case of poor concentration, but specifically in the case of learning difficulties. This conclusion is further supported by the work of Colin Wilsher et al. (editor): *Developmental Dyslexia and Learning Disorders. Diagnosis and Treatment*, Vol. 5 of the series *Child Health and Development*, Paris, 1987 (publisher: Karger). Saviour P. and Ramachanra N.B. Biological basis of dyslexia: A maturing perspective. Current science. 75 Jan **2006**. vol. 90, No.2.pp:168-175. xxxiii. Conners, C.K. and Schulte, A.C. Learning

What you need to consider

Competent professional support is crucial if medication is to be successful. You need a doctor who has been well trained in this field, is knowledgeable in this respect and can provide evidence of success.

If a diagnosis has been made, treatment begins with a very small dose (as it is best to be on the safe side) in the morning. This remains ineffective in the majority of cases. The dosage is gradually increased until the child's symptoms are reduced. Children often fail to notice any improvement in the beginning, which is why the observations of parents and educators are extremely important. If the specialist considers an optimum dose has been achieved, this is then maintained and adhered to for the whole day to achieve the best possible results in terms of attentiveness and behaviour and, as you now know, maturation of the relevant brain region.

During this maturation process, your child may again appear inattentive, restless, and depressed. In this case, the experienced practitioner knows that the dose should be reduced. Step by step, the treatment continues in this manner until the desired maturation has been achieved and medicament can be completely discontinued.

It is important to note that children can react with differing degrees of sensitivity to the variety of medications and the active ingredients involved, meaning it is equally important to determine the most suitable active ingredient by conducting several tests where necessary.

Individual dosage

The metabolism of the brain differs from child to child, as does the degree of immaturity of the brain region that controls attentiveness. Your child or adolescent is in the midst of a dynamic learning and growth process, which is why it is crucial to find the appropriate dosage for each individual. This can be very low in exceptional cases (perhaps only a quarter of the usual 10 mg tablet), but also high in others. A brief anecdote illustrates this well. At an ADHD symposium which we organised in Tuttlingen; a well-known expert told a story about a grandmother who had forgotten his instructions concerning the amount of medicine. When asked during a check-up how her grandson was now faring, she replied, "Thank you, Doctor, he's fine. He takes his eight tablets every day, and he's really getting on great now!"

Other experienced physicians also report the achievement of very good results through individual dosage, even when this is higher than the norm. On the other hand, it is not uncommon for your child to show no reaction to the medicine, purely because the dosage is too low (probably due to ignorance or exaggerated cautiousness).

Disadvantages of medication

Medicines such as *Ritalin*, *Medikinet* and, to a lesser degree, *Piracetam* are stimulants similar to amphetamine, and they can have a powerful impact.

Unfortunately, the public perception of medical treatment is often coloured by negative reporting. Horror stories about ADHD treatment producing confused, overdosed children repeatedly circulate in the media. In fact, it is often the case that the initial dose administered is too high and your child reacts negatively (as in an extremely apathetic reaction). An experienced doctor then immediately lowers the dose until the ideal dosage for your child is determined.

The word is: always begin low.

Monitoring the intake of medication

Medication needs be taken regularly throughout the day. Problems arise when a child forgets to take the tablet in school or deliberately neglects to because it is embarrassing in front of classmates. Some children simply do not want to take the tablets. Delayed-release dosage has improved this situation today, with the capsule being taken in the morning and the active substance releasing slowly up until noon. This delayed-release dosage form may need to be additionally supported by conventional tablets or parts thereof to achieve the optimum effect.

Side effects of methylphenidate

Despite care and a very gradual increase in the dosage, side effects may be experienced. Many children lose their appetite until the effect of the drug fades in the evening. Experts therefore recommend moving the family's main meal to the evening. The drug is still working if children are still not hungry in the evening and, in this case, the dosage should be checked again and fine tuning undertaken. Sometimes the dosage is no longer sufficient to increase the ability to concentrate, but still so strong that it suppresses any feeling of hunger.

Insomnia is frequently cited as a side-effect, which is also a reason for adjusting the dosage so that the effect abates in the evening. Should this prove inadequate, a trial with other medicines is a sensible decision. As already described above, Dr Held believed that *Piracetam* is very effective in encouraging maturation of the ability to concentrate – without side effects.

There is also a risk of possible abuse of medication, as reports of ADHD medicines being taken as intoxicants are not an infrequent occurrence.

Positive side effects

Apart from the fact that children generally react very favourably when the drug is successfully introduced and due to the improved level of attentiveness and behaviour achieved, a number of further positive developments should also be mentioned. It has been observed that the area of motor activity improves, an example being in the maturation of muscle tone. As a consequence, the bladder muscles function as they should, and bedwetting ceases.

In addition, parents report time and again that their child can now *draw* accurately or is suddenly able to cut straight along a line with scissors, something they never succeeded in mastering previously. Writing also usually improves very quickly – to the teacher's (and everyone else's) relief.

Improvements in social maturity and both literacy and arithmetic skills are achieved. I am often invited by ADHD experts at this point to demonstrate how the remaining "residue" of dyslexia and dyscalculia can be overcome. Other positive side effects include maturation of the immune system and the reduction of autoimmune symptoms such as neurodermatitis or hay fever.

To conclude, it should be pointed out that not all children respond to treatment with such stimulants, and about 20 per cent fail to react at all to this therapy.

Audio-visual stimulation

In this method, stimulation occurs while listening to "coded" impulse recordings which underlay relaxing music. The recordings are made on CDs or mp3 files. These special sound impulses are sent to the brain of your child, activating those brain waves that are also generated when we feel comfortable, relaxed, friendly and creative. In short, children become more relaxed and focussed through the improved distribution of relevant neurotransmitters in the brain.

In addition, musical sound impulses can actually be *seen* with the aid of special glasses! In a study of the Mind's Eye Plus audio-visual program in 1990, Bruce Harrah-Conforth noted that test individuals also generated alpha waves without sound impulses through visual stimulation with special LED-equipped glasses.

"Ski goggles" of this kind are equipped with small light-emitting diodes that transmit light pulses to the closed eyelids. Users of good products usually report that the image patterns generated are pleasant, colourful and diverse. What is important for you and your child is that your child's brain is stimulated as a result and with increasing intensity. Stimulation is the key to success in your efforts to overcome your child's poor concentration and/or hyperactivity!

Advantages of audio-visual stimulation

The device and CDs and mp3s are very easy to handle and versatile in their application. Your child can lie on the sofa after school and enjoy the benefits of an AVS session. In addition to homework and our concept for overcoming dyslexia, you can also run an AVS CD in the background. During lessons in the *Kennedy Tutorial School*, we compared exercises with and without a CD and found that children concentrated better with a CD in the background, being less restless than without CD music.

Due to the frequency with which sleep disturbances are encountered in ADHD children, it is recommended that children be allowed to enjoy a thirty-minute session in bed. Don't forget to look in after this time and take the headphones and glasses off your sleeping child.

If the audio-visual method is applied regularly, the positive results achieved with very little effort are extremely convincing. These have been proven in scientific studies which demonstrate an effect as positive as with Ritalin. For example, Harold L. Russell conducted numerous investigations into the long-term effectiveness of AVS on schoolchildren between 1994 and 1996 at the University of Texas. The positive effect is most evident in everyday practice, and we frequently receive feedback from parents who say that their children can concentrate better, are more attentive, feel better and, in almost all cases, sleep sounder and without interruptions.

Audio-visual stimulation is an extremely practicable complement to alphabetic training which can be easily integrated into everyday life.

Disadvantages of audio-visual stimulation

- The visual application is unsuitable for epilepsy sufferers, due to the flickering LED lights employed.

- A gradual, step-by-step approach needs to be adopted with very sensitive children. The length and intensity of the application (sound and light intensity) are gradually increased.

- Your child should use the application for 20 to 30 minutes daily, which is why a wide selection of good music tracks is required.

Behavioural training

The behaviour of ADHD children and adolescents can be greatly improved by forging agreements developed together on how they should behave in different situations. With the aid of an experienced specialist who structures the entire daily routine together with child and parents, this approach can be very effective.

This not only involves discussing how your child should behave, but also the reaction of parents and educators in the event of misconduct on the part of the child. Assistance is also offered. For example, posters are created with your child and placed around the house, indicating what should be done during the morning, at noon and in the evening. In addition to cleaning teeth, setting the table and clearing away the school bag, this can also include the condition in which the bathroom should be left, when homework is to be done, when TV can be watched, when to go to bed and what to do beforehand.

Rules of play are also developed for communication within the family. Finally, measures to be taken following misconduct are agreed.

This gives both your child and family a greater sense of security and a *framework* in which they can move with confidence. Many ADHD experts recommend behavioural training of this nature in addition to medication.

Disadvantages of behavioural training

Behavioural training is an effort-intensive approach and, as always when bringing up children, demands a lot of stamina, determination and assertiveness. These days there are courses for parents wishing to hone and improve their skills in dealing with their ADHD child. The *effects* of ADHD can thus be reduced to a minimum, depending on the particular case and severity – but not the symptoms, which your child will continue to exhibit.

My recommendation for you

This book has helped you to determine whether your child has dyslexia or dyscalculia or not, and possibly if it also affected by ADHD. Should there be any suspicion of ADHD, scrutinise your child three times with our online test and find an experienced ADHD doctor to clarify whether your assumption is justified. Include examples from everyday life to back up your suspicion. In addition to home life, these should also include school and the observations of relatives and friends. Describe, using examples, your child's struggle with this disorder from early on, including infancy, nursery or kindergarten and the present. The doctor can then advise you on appropriate measures.

Parent initiatives where families affected by ADHD advise and support each other are extremely useful. Many of these parents have had similar experiences to you, frequently undertaking a very lengthy journey before they resolved their problem. You can benefit from their experience and significantly shorten your road to an effective solution. Parent initiatives in your region can be found on the internet. Put in your town and the term adhd parents' initiative, for example *parents ini adhd Tamworth Staffs England*
or *www.chadd.org > find a local chadd USA*

ADHD is worrying for both parents and children, especially if it occurs in addition to dyslexia and/or dyscalculia - *which is the rule rather than the exception.* But if you and your child remain resolute, practice with letters and quantities and meticulously apply the remedial measures for ADHD appropriate for your child, the affected brain regions will develop and mature, they always do! Your child can overcome their difficulties within a year.

So, let's get down to work! Believe me, you can do it!

Postscript:

"That's enough for the moment. Time to play now ...!"

Leo, please come up here to me."

Leo moved very slowly towards Herr Schalldecker, his class teacher at the front of the room. As he was about to get his mark in German in his end-of-year report for sixth class, he really was in no hurry.

"Don't worry, Leo. You've got a 2 in German, and you've really earned it! You've made enormous progress since last year. Your essays have also improved greatly, and I really enjoy reading them. Just in case you're not sure what you'd like to do later, I'd strongly suggest you try writing professionally. You're making significantly fewer spelling mistakes, and your mother told me that you're reading one book after another at home. Okay, that's enough for the moment. Time to play now ...!"

Leo was practically bursting with pride as he told me what his teacher had said. And goodness knows he was entitled to be! Only a year earlier he had been utterly desperate, and his mother also despaired of seeing any improvement. He was practising and learning every day at this time, but nothing he did seemed to lead to an improvement in his marks. And now, thanks to playing with the letters of the alphabet - finally, the breakthrough had come.

Dyslexia can always be conquered, and the road to success need not be stressful, as it involves exercises that children enjoy. The prerequisite for this is that the problem should be clearly identified and your child given the opportunity to imprint letters using all its senses. Systematically and regularly.

Please do not forget that the homework your child gets is intended for children who do not suffer from any learning difficulties. This is precisely why *our* typing exercise and games described in this book should take *priority* in your child's daily school life.

And always remember, it pays to persevere and stay on course!

Please write to me and tell me about your child's experience and success using our method, as I would be very happy to hear from you.

Dedication and thanks

My purpose in writing this book has been to help all parents and children who are desperately trying to overcome dyslexia. And more recently, to reach out to progressive open-minded schools which are flexible enough to incorporate these methods on a daily basis to improve the lives of all their charges. And also, to measurably increase their own school's standing in the community with regard to achieving true literacy, numeracy and cognition.

With this in mind, I would like to express my thanks to my colleagues at the *Kennedy Tutorial School* and in the *Kreatives Lernen* educational mail-order department for their professionalism in implementing the Individual Development Program.

With regard to professionalism, I would also like to thank posthumously Herbert Leger for his excellent contributions regarding motivation and conversational skills!

Last but not least, my gratitude to my wife and family for the support they have given me over the years.

And also, for the late Dr Held, I would like to dedicate this quotation from Barbara Tuchman:

"Without books, history is silent, literature dumb, science crippled, thought and speculation at a standstill. They are engines of change …, windows on the world …. They are … bankers of the treasures of the mind. Books are humanity in print."

Joseph Kennedy

About the Author

Joe's passion has always been about learning. In 1975 he decided to move from England to Germany. He found not only his new home in the small town of Tuttlingen, but also developed the Individual Development Program (IDP) which is revolutionizing the tutorial market in Germany.

Since then, Joe, author and teacher, has been helping many families whose children have learning disabilities and behavioural challenges. Joe Kennedy shows children, teenagers and parents alternative methods of achieving measurable accomplishment and: success is fun!

Joe's credo is: "No child is unintelligent"

More recently he has turned to helping schools at home and abroad as an educational consultant.

In private life Joe enjoys time with his family and five little grandchildren. Reading is his passion and he enjoys visiting art galleries every now and then.

https://joekennedy-education-consultant.com/

j.kennedy@crealern.de

Printed in Great Britain
by Amazon